CONTEMPORARY LESBIAN WRITING

GENDER IN WRITING

Series Editor: Kate Flint
University Lecturer in Victorian and Modern English Literature,
Faculty of English, Oxford University

Difference in language, in subject matter, in form. This series seeks to explore what is distinctive about women's and men's writing, and to examine the theories of sexuality which attempt to explain these differences. Writings of all periods and genres will be looked at from a variety of radical perspectives: some explicitly feminist, others examining masculinity, homosexuality and gender politics as they are constructed through the writing and reading of texts. The series will draw on recent developments in literary theory in order to examine all aspects of gender in writing.

Published Titles:

British and Irish Women Dramatists since 1958
Trevor R. Griffiths and Margaret Llewellyn-Jones (eds)

Writing for Women: The Example of Woman as Reader in Elizabethan Romance
Caroline Lucas

Gender in Irish Writing
Toni O'Brien Johnson and David Cairns (eds)

Contemporary Lesbian Writing: Dreams, Desire, Difference
Paulina Palmer

Writing Differences: Readings from the Seminar of Hélène Cixous
Susan Sellers (ed.)

CONTEMPORARY LESBIAN WRITING

Dreams, desire, difference

PAULINA PALMER

OPEN UNIVERSITY PRESS
BUCKINGHAM · PHILADELPHIA

Open University Press
Celtic Court
22 Ballmoor
Buckingham
MK18 1XW

and
1900 Frost Road, Suite 101
Bristol, PA 19007, USA

First Published 1993

A catalogue record of this book is available from the British Library

ISBN 0 335 09038 9 (pb)   0 335 09039 7 (hb)

Library of Congress Cataloging-in-Publication Data

Palmer, Paulina, 1937–
    Contemporary lesbian writing : dreams, desire, difference / by
Paulina Palmer.
        p.   cm. — (Gender in writing)
    Includes bibliographical references (p.) and index.
    ISBN 0-335-09039-7. — ISBN 0-335-09038-9 (pbk.)
    1. Lesbian writings, American—History and criticism.   2. Women
and literature—United States—History—20th century.   3. Women and
literature—Great Britain—History—20th century.   4. American
literature—20th century—History and criticism.   5. English
literature—20th century—History and criticism.   6. Lesbian
writings, English—History and criticism.   7. Lesbians in
literature.   I. Title.   II. Series.
PS153.L46P35   1993
810.8'09206643—dc20   93-2467
                                                               CIP

Typeset by Inforum, Rowlands Castle, Hants.
Printed in Great Britain by St Edmundsbury Press,
Bury St Edmunds, Suffolk

For Cambridge Lesbian Line

Contents

Preface and acknowledgements

Gone are the days when a book on the topic of lesbian writing could be expected to appeal only to those readers who identify as lesbian or bisexual. With lesbian fiction and theory assuming an increasingly prominent place in Women's Studies and in the study of contemporary literature and criticism, its readership is likely to be notably more diverse. *Contemporary Lesbian Writing: Dreams, Desire, Difference* is intended for a variety of different readers. Students and teachers of Lesbian Studies and Women's Studies, along with those working in the field of literature in general, will, I hope, find it useful. Non-academic readers who enjoy lesbian fiction and seek to learn more about its cultural and theoretical context may also find it interesting. Contemporary lesbian writing is a topic which has started to receive recognition only in the past few years. Several British critics have recently edited collections of essays referring to it and the American Bonnie Zimmerman has published her critical study *The Safe Sea of Women: Lesbian Fiction 1969–1989*. However my book is one of the first by a British author to focus on lesbian writing.

The idea of producing this book has been with me for some time. Essays on lesbian/feminist fiction and theory, which I have written in the past few years, have contributed towards it. So too have certain papers which I have given at American and British conferences. Ideas frequently emerge in interaction with other people, and I am indebted to friends and colleagues in this respect. I am particularly grateful for the encouragement and support of Christine Battersby and Gill Frith, with whom I teach undergraduate and graduate courses at the University of Warwick. I am also indebted to

Sonya Andermahr for helping to keep me up to date with new trends in lesbian writing and alerting my attention to new publications. The various students who, over the past few years, have attended the courses on feminist writing and critical theory which I teach at Warwick, have also played a vital part. Some of them have chosen to focus their essays and dissertations on lesbian topics – and I have found discussion with them intellectually stimulating. Lesbian writing, although it is increasingly significant, is not exactly at the centre of the curriculum in British colleges and universities. Teaching it tends to be tolerated rather than encouraged. I'm thus pleased when the occasional student or colleague shows an interest in lesbian texts and ideas and indicates a wish to discuss them.

As well as valuing the interest and encouragement of friends, colleagues and students, I am also indebted to certain historians and critics who work in the field of Lesbian Studies. Lillian Faderman and Bonnie Zimmerman are particularly important in this respect. Though not always agreeing with their points of view or interpretation of texts or events, I have found their books and essays an invaluable source of knowledge and information. Reference to their ideas occurs frequently in the following pages.

Here it is necessary to explain the procedural method which I employ regarding the dating and editions of the theoretical and fictional works to which I refer. Many of these have been published in different editions by different publishing houses. On first mentioning a particular text, I cite the initial date of publication. In quoting from it, however, I frequently use a later edition (generally the British one, if it is available) and give details of it in a note. Details of both are to be found in the Bibliography.

1

Introduction

Although now I'm publishing with a mainstream publisher, reviewed in the mainstream press, I'm not a valued person. I'm a deviant person. Reviews that I now get say things like 'This isn't a gay book, this is a universal book.' That's called a good review; because if it was a gay book there'd be something wrong with it.

(Sarah Schulman 1992: 222)

In the past two decades, since the advent of the Lesbian Feminist Movement in the early 1970s, lesbian writing has aroused an unprecedented degree of interest. As is apparent from publishers' lists and the sections of bookshops focusing on Feminist Studies and Gender Studies, it can no longer be seen as a unitary category but encompasses a variety of different discourses and perspectives – sociological, theoretical, critical and literary. Some examples of lesbian writing are intended to cater for an academic readership for, with the growth of Women's Studies and Lesbian Studies in colleges and universities, texts of this kind are starting to appear in the curriculum. Others, however, are written for non-academic readers. This is particularly the case with fiction which, with writers such as Mary Wings,[1] Joanna Russ[2] and Ellen Galford[3] appropriating and reworking the popular genres of the thriller, science fiction and Gothic, is widely read. The success which lesbian writing is currently enjoying, though certainly welcome, gives rise to contradictions. For example, as the passage from Schulman's 'Troubled Times' which prefaces this chapter illustrates, lesbian texts tend to be valued by mainstream critics not for their lesbian content but for 'universal' features such as an understanding of human experience and portrayal of character.[4] Contradictions are also apparent in the field of lesbian writing itself. One of the most obvious is that, while the theoretical works produced by exponents of poststructuralism such as Judith Butler and Eve Kosofsky Sedgwick are becoming increasingly intellectually and stylistically obscure and esoteric and appeal to a minority academic readership, lesbian fiction, on account of its utilization of popular genres and their conventions, is easily accessible and is enjoyed by women of all kinds.[5]

This study discusses both the academic and the popular strands of lesbian writing. Theory and fiction, the two categories on which it focuses, display a number of significant modifications and developments which merit investigation. In the field of theory, the representation of lesbianism as the signifier of feminism and the association of it with the concept of woman-identification, which were accepted in the 1970s, have been challenged. Its sexual dimension now receives greater recognition. Desire and its connections with fantasy, along with a lesbian erotics, are topics of enquiry. Lesbian Studies, moreover, are no longer assumed to be a branch of Women's Studies but are in the process of becoming a separate discipline. The idea of a unitary lesbian identity and the representation of lesbians as a homogeneous group have also been problematized. In discussing the latter, theorists concentrate attention on the importance of *difference*. They highlight not only differences between lesbians and heterosexual women, as was the case in the 1970s, but also those between lesbians.[6]

In the field of fiction significant changes have also occurred. Here again 'difference' and 'desire' are supplanting 'identification' and 'politics' as key ideas. With the advent of lesbian genre fiction, the view of the lesbian novel as a unitary entity has been replaced by a focus on fiction of different kinds. Writers such as Elizabeth Riley[7] and Nancy Toder,[8] working in the 1970s, concentrate, somewhat narrowly, on the theme of Coming Out. In recent years, however, a variety of different genres and kinds have emerged, including the thriller and the comic novel. The stories of Jane DeLynn[9] and the novels of Schulman[10] focus explicitly on sex; they explore issues of topical interest, such as different cultural constructs of lesbianism, butch and femme identification, and the effects of the AIDS crisis on the gay community. This diversification has brought about important changes in critical perspectives. Critics working in the field of lesbian literary studies, rather than seeking to define a single lesbian style and aesthetic, as they did in the past,[11] acknowledge the existence of a variety of different styles and approaches. Examples of realism, fantasy and anti-realism flourish side by side. In some novels, such as Jeanette Winterson's *Oranges Are Not the Only Fruit* (1985), they co-exist and intermingle.

As well as concentrating attention on theory and fiction as separate categories, this study also explores the interaction which takes place between them. This is illustrated by the way writers of fiction appropriate ideas from theoretical discourse and, by employing them as the intellectual base for their texts, rework them in narrative form. To investigate this, I open the book with a chapter discussing aspects of theory and follow it with four chapters focusing on fiction of different kinds. Here, I pick up the ideas which I introduced earlier, examining the role which they play in novels and stories. In discussing the interplay between fiction and theory, as

I do in these chapters, I develop the line of thought which I pursued in my previously published study, *Contemporary Women's Fiction: Narrative Practice and Feminist Theory* (1989). This refers to a number of lesbian texts, and here I develop some of the perceptions which I arrived at there.

In considering works of lesbian theory and fiction, and the interaction between them, I concentrate attention on texts by both American and British writers. Instead of assigning these to different chapters, I have decided to interrelate references to them. While this may occasionally result in obscuring differences stemming from geography and nationality, it has the advantage of highlighting their political and ideological affinities. It also gives scope for comparison and contrast. A notable feature of contemporary lesbian writing is the way that, on account of the influence of the Lesbian Movement and its perspectives, genres such as the Coming Out novel, the comic novel, and fiction centering on the lesbian community, while differing in certain respects in North America and the United Kingdom, are popular in both countries.

My interest in exploring the varied strands in lesbian writing, as well as being an intellectual one, reflects the disparate areas of lesbian culture and social life in which I'm involved at present. As well as teaching at a British university where I hold seminars on lesbian theory for the Women's Studies MA and supervise students writing essays and dissertations on lesbian topics, I am also a member of the local lesbian help-line in my home town. Here too an interest in lesbian writing is apparent, though of a less specialized kind. The callers who phone the Line sometimes ask us to recommend books on different facets of lesbianism. In addition, the Line has a box of books (fiction, mostly) which we read and lend out. Women living in outlying rural areas find them particularly useful. These books, as well as being a source of entertainment, provide a cultural context which endorses our orientation, offering us support and reassurance. A feature of lesbian existence which I find difficult to convey to friends who identify as heterosexual is the degree of isolation and alienation which many lesbians experience on account of the heterosexist bias of the media, press and education system. Reading lesbian fiction, both popular and otherwise, helps in a small way to compensate for this.

Several different factors serve to account for the vitality of lesbian writing at the present time and the success which it is enjoying. On a commercial level, the growth of feminist publishing houses, such as the Women's Press and Virago, have promoted its circulation. Specifically lesbian publishing houses, such as the North American Naiad and the British Onlywomen, and houses which place an emphasis on lesbian writing, such as the recently established Scarlet Press, also play a vital role. On an intellectual plane, the contested nature of the sign *lesbian* and the debates which it has provoked have brought lesbianism to the attention of the general public. The sign is a controversial one, with right-wing moralists, merchants of porn, lesbian feminists and lesbian sexual radicals each attempting to define it and impose on it their own meaning. Debate takes place not only between pro-lesbian and anti-lesbian factions but also, as we shall see, among lesbians themselves. They frequently disagree about the precise significance of the sign and the issues relating to it. Is it solely sexual in import or is it also political? Are lesbian studies best pursued in the context of feminism or is such a frame restrictive? Is it possible to speak of a unitary lesbian identity and to see women who identify as lesbian as a homogeneous group? Is 'identification' or 'difference' the motivating impulse of lesbian attraction and desire? And what about the lesbian herself? Is she the deviant, erotically transgressive figure associated with 'the underworld, the underground, the unconscious . . . the excitement of danger'[12] whom Elizabeth Wilson admits haunts her imagination and who is portrayed in Schulman's *After Delores* (1988) and the stories of DeLynn, or is she, on the contrary, the heroic, politically right-on feminist who leads her sisters to challenge male oppression, as Jill does in Piercy's *Small Changes* (1972) and Sandy in Toder's *Choices* (1980)? Is she a combination of both these stereotypes? Is each, perhaps, applicable in a different cultural situation and at a different period of lesbian history?[13]

These questions recur in the texts discussed below, creating a linking thread and indicating the existence of a tradition of writing which, having come to the fore in the 1970s, continues to develop and acquire new facets. Lesbian writing itself, the subject of this study, is, of course, another term which raises questions. As has been brought to my attention at conferences where questioners have queried my use of the category, it is problematic. Does it denote writing by lesbians, for lesbians, or about lesbians? As I argue elsewhere,[14] none of these definitions is entirely satisfactory or foolproof. In the 1970s the concept of lesbian writing was less contentious – among lesbians themselves at least. It gained validity from the concept of the lesbian writer, a figure with feminist allegiances who addresses her texts to the lesbian community, promoted by the Lesbian Feminist Movement.[15] However, with poststructuralist thought questioning the author's role as the controlling principle of the text, this definition has become controversial. Moreover, how are we to define a novel such as Winterson's *Sexing the Cherry* (1989) which, though written by a woman who identifies as lesbian, refers to a variety of different sexual identifications and is addressed to a general readership? As I argue in Chapter 6, where I discuss it, the themes and motifs which it treats (the problematization of heterosexual relations and the subversive reworking of the image of woman as monster) are central to the lesbian literary tradition and thus merit attention here. However, the novel certainly highlights the problems of definition which confront the critic.

None the less the concept of lesbian writing and a lesbian literary tradition, despite their fluidity and imprecision, continue to flourish. They are enabling culturally and politically since, as well as providing a context in which writers and readers can work, they help to preserve lesbianism from invisibility. They also promote a spirit of community among lesbians and challenge homophobic and phallocentric attitudes. In relation to the latter I need to point out that lesbian fiction of political protest, far from being defunct as some critics imply,[16] is very much alive. Examples of it include Schulman's *People in Trouble* (1990), which exposes the public lack of concern about the AIDS crisis, and Galford's *Queendom Come* (1990), which takes as its target of attack the notorious Section 28 and its oppressive effects.[17] These novels are less separatist in emphasis than those of Piercy, Russ and other writers of the 1970s and, in contrast to them, treat issues of importance to the lesbian and gay community as a whole. However, they display a similar degree of political vigour.

Lesbian writing does not exist in a vacuum but is closely linked to the social and political circumstances which form its context. Here, in the 1990s, contradictions are also apparent. In the realms of publishing and the academy the situation gives cause for optimism. Lesbian and Gay Studies are growth areas, and courses[18] and conferences[19] focusing on them are increasingly common. In the university department of literature where I teach, although accusations of 'proselytizing' and trite jokes about the danger of lesbians 'taking over' are occasionally voiced, I and my gay male colleague enjoy the support of some members of staff, and feel relatively free to introduce lesbian and gay topics into our courses. In other areas, however, the situation is less positive. Not only have the liberatory aims of the Lesbian and Gay Movement failed to be achieved but also the pressures of the recession, combined with the homophobic backlash of the 1980s, have led, in some cases, to their erosion. British and American lesbian communities continue to flourish, represented by help-lines, activist groups, study groups and social networks. However, Coming Out to employers, co-workers, landlords and relatives has become more difficult. Many women I know have ceased to regard it as a practical goal and resign themselves, as far as their contact with heterosexuals is concerned, to leading closeted lives. Whereas lip-service is paid in many professions to equal opportunities in race and gender, sexual orientation seldom enjoys even this meagre tribute. In fact, the introduction of Section 28 in 1988 has given discrimination against lesbians and gay men in the United Kingdom a new respectability. The Section, though intimidatory in nature rather than explicitly prescriptive,[20] has resulted in the withdrawal of funding from help-lines and social centres and led to the cancellation of gay cultural events.[21] It has also had an adverse effect on lesbian and gay schoolchildren for, as a former teacher and barrister observes, 'It was designed to put the frighteners on teachers, schools and education authorities'[22] by discouraging the discussion of homosexuality. Incidents of queer-bashing and attempted suicide among schoolchildren are on the increase, and ostracism and verbal abuse are 'getting worse'.[23] Another target of the Section is, of course, lesbian mothers. It discriminates overtly against them by describing their families as 'pretended'.[24]

This gloomy picture of suffering and oppression makes the increasing division between the academic and popular aspects of lesbian thought and culture, mentioned above, particularly worrying. As Bonnie Zimmerman observes, 'The discourses of "common sense" and contemporary theory seem to be moving further and further apart.' Maybe the time has come for us to confront this rift and its implications and discuss the question she raises: 'What is the responsibility of the critic and the theorist to the writer, to the text, and to the community of readers?'[25]

Despite, or possibly because of, the stigmatization and prejudice which they frequently encounter, and the discrepancy between the actual and the ideal which their situation illustrates, women who identify as lesbian and the texts which they produce often display a preoccupation with fantasy. The pegs on which we hang our dreams vary from era to era. In the 1970s and the early 1980s lesbian feminist identity and community, and the challenges which they direct at patriarchal power, were important ideals. In the 1990s, with sexuality and psychoanalysis assuming prominence in Lesbian Studies, we are starting to investigate the workings of fantasy itself. The imaginary scenarios which women create, the images they project on one another, and the psychological significance of different sexual identifications and practices are topics of enquiry.[26]

Lesbian fiction, too, reveals an interest in fantasy, one which, though encompassing the topic of sex, extends beyond it. From the 1970s onwards fantasy themes and modes of writing have played a key role in novels and stories. They include the pastoral utopianism of Sally Miller Gearhart's *The Wanderground* (1979), which juxtaposes images of the city and the country and represents women's community in a celebratory light; the humorous interplay between materials from Hindu myth and the comments voiced by an exceptionally articulate Brahmin ruminant in Suniti Namjoshi's *The Conversations of Cow* (1985); and the reworking of fairy tales and fables in Winterson's novels. These, along with other dreams and fantasies which contribute to lesbian culture, are discussed in the chapters ahead.

Notes

1 Wings, *She Came Too Late* (Women's Press, 1986).
2 Russ, *The Female Man* (Bantam, 1975).
3 Galford, *The Fires of Bride* (Women's Press, 1986).
4 See Hilary Hinds's discussion of the reception of Jeanette Winterson's *Oranges Are Not the Only Fruit* in Sally Munt (ed.), *New Lesbian Criticism: Literary and Cultural Readings* (Harvester Wheatsheaf, 1992), pp. 153–72.

5 Bonnie Zimmerman comments on the division between academic and popular perspectives on lesbianism in 'Lesbians Like This and That: Some Notes on Lesbian Criticism for the Nineties', in *New Lesbian Criticism*, ed. cit., pp. 12–13.

6 For references to these topics see Chapter 2, pp. 22–31. See also Lillian Faderman, *Odd Girls and Twilight Lovers: A History of Lesbian Life in Twentieth-Century America* (Penguin, 1992), pp. 246–302; and Sedgwick, *Epistemology of the Closet* (Harvester Wheatsheaf, 1991), pp. 35–9.

7 Riley, *All That False Instruction* (Angus and Robertson, 1975; Sirius Quality Paperback, 1981).

8 Toder, *Choices* (Persephone Press, 1980).

9 De Lynn, *Don Juan in the Village* (Serpent's Tail, 1991).

10 Schulman, *After Delores* (Sheba, 1990) and Schulman, *People in Trouble* (Sheba, 1990).

11 See Zimmerman, 'What Has Never Been: An Overview of Lesbian Feminist Criticism', in Gayle Greene and Coppelia Kahn (eds) *Making a Difference: Feminist Literary Criticism* (Methuen, 1985), pp. 194–7.

12 Wilson with Weir, *Hidden Agendas: Theory, Politics and Experience in the Women's Movement* (Tavistock, 1986), p. 181.

13 For discussion of these questions see Chapter 2, pp. 14–31.

14 Palmer, 'Contemporary Lesbian Feminist Fiction: Texts for Everywoman', in Linda Anderson (ed.) *Plotting Change: Contemporary Women's Fiction* (Edward Arnold, 1990), pp. 44–6.

15 Zimmerman discusses this in *The Safe Sea of Women: Lesbian Fiction 1969–1989* (Onlywomen, 1992), p. 15.

16 See Zimmerman, *The Safe Sea of Women*, ed. cit., pp. 208–20.

17 Section 28 of the Local Government Act was sponsored by a group of Tory backbenchers and, despite considerable opposition, came into force in the United Kingdom on 24 May 1988. It prohibits local authorities from: a) promoting homosexuality or publishing material that promotes homosexuality; b) promoting the teaching in maintained schools of homosexuality as a pretended family relationship; or c) giving financial assistance to any person for either of these purposes. As Duncan Fallowell points out, it has given 'official approval to homophobia in the country at large' (*The Guardian*, 1 December 1989, p. 36). For discussion of Section 28 and its significance see Madeleine Colvin with Jane Hawksley, *Section 28: A Practical Guide to the Law and its Implications* (National Council for Civil Liberties, 1989).

18 British universities, including Warwick, have run undergraduate courses in Lesbian and Gay Studies. The University of Sussex has an MA in Sexual Dissidence and Cultural Change. Students report that the latter, in its present (1992–3) format, is not entirely successful. However, it is, none the less, important in helping to initiate Lesbian and Gay Studies in the United Kingdom.

19 British conferences include the two 'Questions of Homosexuality' Conferences (University of London, 1991 and 1992) and the 'Activating Theory' Conference (University of York, 1992).

20 See Sarah Roelof's feature in *Spare Rib*, 192 (June 1988), p. 42.

21 See Colvin and Hawksley, op. cit., pp. 52–5.

22 A comment made by Simon Harris, the author of *Lesbian and Gay Issues in the English Classroom* (Open University Press), cited by Neil McKenna in his feature on homosexuality in the classroom in *The Guardian*, 25 November 1991, p. 14.

23 Neil McKenna, op. cit., p. 14. New guidelines on Sex Education in schools, recently issued by the British Government, which outlaw the representing of homosexuality in a sympathetic light, also increase the pressure on lesbian and gay pupils, contributing to their oppression.

24 See the feature by Scarlett McGuire in *The Guardian*, 25 April 1988, p. 16.

25 Zimmerman, 'Lesbians Like This and That', ed. cit., p. 13.

26 Essays focusing on these topics include Jessica Benjamin, 'Master and Slave: The Fantasy of Erotic Domination', in Ann Snitow, Christine Stansell and Sharon Thompson (eds) *Desire: The Politics of Sexuality* (Virago, 1984), pp. 292–311; Stephanie Castendyk, 'A Psychoanalytic Account for Lesbianism', *Feminist Review*, 42 (1992), pp. 67–81; and Diane Hamer, 'Significant Others: Lesbians and Psychoanalytic Theory', *Feminist Review,* 34 (1990), pp. 134–51.

2

Theoretical perspectives

The only thing for certain is how complicated it all is, like a string full of knots. It's all there but hard to find the beginning and impossible to fathom the end. The best you can do is admire the cat's cradle and maybe knot it up a bit more.

(Jeanette Winterson 1985: 93)

The Lesbian Feminist Movement and its development

The emergence of the initial documents of the Lesbian Feminist Movement, such as Radicalesbians' 'The Woman Identified Woman' (1970) and Ti-Grace Atkinson's 'Lesbianism and Feminism' (1972), in the early 1970s has something of an air of magic about it. To the reader unacquainted with lesbian history they appear to have materialized out of thin air like the conjuror's proverbial egg. This impression is encouraged by the tendency of commentators to discuss the ideas which they treat out of context, ignoring the social and historical factors which form their background.[1] This sometimes works to the essays' advantage, resulting in emphasis being placed on their originality. More often, however, particularly in the present era of the 1990s, when political perspectives on lesbianism are being supplanted by libertarian ones and the analysis of sex and gender has become more intellectually complex, it works against them. Readers ignore the experimental nature of these early works, as well as the social and political issues which they address. They misunderstand their aims and expect them to display a knowledge of theory and psychoanalysis which was not available at the time they were written. To read them fairly and understand their true significance, we need to know something about their circumstances of publication. This enables us to appreciate the impressive challenge which they directed at the homophobic attitudes of the period.

Many of these early essays, whether signed by a collective or an individual, originated in the context of group discussion. They created the basis for a lesbian sexual politics, by making an intervention in the feminist agenda and questioning and problematizing heterosexist assumptions. The stranglehold which heterosexism exerted on the female psyche in the early days of the Women's Liberation Movement is illustrated by the comments voiced by the members of a London-based consciousness-raising group. Looking back on their early meetings, they admit that, while questioning woman's role in society and challenging male oppression in many areas of life, they took for granted their heterosexual orientation, regarding it as natural and immutable. One woman recalls:

> We talked for hours about sex, problems with men, how we resented sex-roles . . . all those kinds of things. But we never wondered how we got to be heterosexual. The question just didn't arise. I suppose, like the rest of the world, we assumed that was the norm. So all our questioning about why a woman's role *within* heterosexuality is constructed in such and such a way, never once extended to questioning heterosexuality itself.[2]

The essays produced in the early years of the Lesbian Feminist Movement, as well as originating in a group context, were addressed to a readership which was, in some respects, communal. They influenced the interests and policy of the numerous lesbian groups and collectives which were then emerging in North America and the United Kingdom. These varied considerably in composition and character; they included consciousness-raising (CR) groups, discussion groups, social caucuses and help-lines. A collection of essays which played a useful role in providing reading material for these burgeoning groups and organizations is the American publication *Radical Feminism* (1973).[3] Its appearance on the shelves of British bookshops was, I remember, an important event. The lesbian discussion groups to which I belonged (it was formed in Cambridge in the mid-1970s as an offshoot of the social group which originated a little earlier) talked over several of the essays it contains. Two of them – Radicalesbians' 'The Woman Identified Woman' (1973: 240–5) and Anne Koedt's 'The Myth of the Vaginal Orgasm' (1973: 198–207) – were to have a formative influence on the Lesbian Feminist Movement and its perspectives. Works such as these, as well as stimulating us intellectually, performed the equally vital function of reassuring us that, in working to create a lesbian counter-culture, we were not alone. If time-travel were a reality and some politically-conscious young lesbian living in the 1990s had flown back across the years to the 1970s to inform us that not only are lesbian identity and community more elusive and ambiguous than we had supposed but also that our efforts to create them would sometimes take place at the expense of other minority groups such as bisexuals, blacks and Asians, we would have been surprised. Those of us who, in the small provincial groups of the seventies, recognized the narrowness of lesbian feminist attitudes sometimes chose to endure them either from lack of alternative companionship or because we did nto wish to jeopardize the fragile links which we were striving to create. On the whole, however, we were so intent on building lesbian community that the possibility that, in attempting to do so, we might generate perspectives which, at a later stage of lesbian history, would be criticized as exclusive and dogmatic seldom crossed our minds.

An attractive feature of lesbian life in the early 1970s, precarious and cliquish though it often was, was the interplay which existed between practice and theory. In 1979 some of the members of the Cambridge groups took the step of transforming the informal system of contact phone-numbers, which we had employed up to then to introduce new members, into a formal help-line. As we could not afford to rent an office, the Line operated for the first few years from the home of one of the members. Despite the problems which we encountered in securing funding and persuading the local papers to accept our advert, the Cambridge Lesbian Line eventually came into being and took its first calls.

Lesbian help-lines,[4] such as the Cambridge one, have received little attention in journals and studies – and their activities remain, on the whole, unrecognized and unrecorded. However, they serve an important practical role. They function as the backbone of the lesbian community by providing a source of help and information on social and cultural events for women who identify as lesbian or bisexual and offering support to those who are in the process of questioning their sexual orientation. They also provide a lifeline for isolated women living in rural areas, as well as for teenagers and married women. The opportunities which these women have for extending their social life, forming new relationships and exploring their sexuality are often limited by family structures and commitments.

Belonging to a lesbian line collective in the 1970s and early 1980s, as well as being a politicizing experience, was intellectually invigorating. Through talking with the women who phoned and meeting them socially, we made connections between the facts of lesbian existence in our provincial home town and its predominantly rural catchment area, and the ideas which we read about in books and essays. Our lesbianism was, in this sense, something shared and communal. We also made links between reading and writing for, in addition to discussing essays, some of us also tried our hand at writing them. Their aim, like those we read in the anthologies which we borrowed or bought, was to articulate connections between lesbianism and feminism, and to create new and positive images – ones which, we hoped, would challenge and supplant the oppressive stereotypes which, as we knew from the difficulty which we experienced in Coming Out to friends and families and the problems we met in trying to find accommodation, dominated public opinion. We were, on the whole, unwilling to talk about sex or discuss a lesbian erotics. Our lack of concern with this would no doubt have astonished the aforementioned time-traveller from the 1990s, provoking expressions of criticism. However, given the bigoted attitudes of the period and the tendency of male sexologists and people in general to regard lesbian-ism solely in terms of sex, it is unsurprising. As Zimmerman comments:

> Lesbians have been reticent and uncomfortable about sexual writing in part because we wish to reject the patriarchal stereotype of the lesbian as a voracious sexual vampire who spends all her time in bed. It is safer to be a lesbian if sex is kept in the closet or under the covers. We don't wish to give the world another stick with which to beat us.[5]

Many of the essays and papers produced in the early days of the Lesbian Feminist Movement did not achieve formal publication but were circulated locally in the newsletters of the newly formed women's centres and lesbian groups or handed round privately among friends. Only the most significant or, possibly, the most fortunate have survived, published in collections such as *Radical Feminism* (Koedt, Levine and Rapone 1973) and *For Lesbians Only* (1988).[6] Both contain material which is primarily American – and I regret that no equivalent collection of British lesbian material exists. This absence, as well as illustrating the fact that lesbian feminist perspectives emerged in the United Kingdom at a slightly later date than in North America, reflects the influence which Socialist Feminism exerted on British feminist publishing in the 1970s. Socialist feminists concentrated chiefly on discussing issues relating to class and economics.[7] Although some of them identified as lesbian, they tended to regard lesbianism not as a political issue but as a matter of personal preference. Some socialist feminists, not content with ignoring its political implications, went so far as to discourage their readers from breaking free from the family structure and forming relation-ships with women on the grounds that to do so was, in their view, 'politi-cally pretty useless'.[8] Hostile influences like this, combined with the lack of interest in lesbianism in the realms of academia and publishing, help to explain why only relatively recently, in the late 1980s and the 1990s, have collections of British lesbian material, such as the admirably comprehensive *Out the Other Side* (1988),[9] started to appear in print.

In seeking to create a lesbian sexual politics and to articulate links be-tween lesbianism and feminism, theorists writing in the 1970s had very little upon which to build. Despite the fact that a number of its members formed involvements with women, the nineteenth-century Women's Movement did not prioritize lesbianism and made little attempt to theorize it. It was, in fact, male sexologists and psychoanalysts who initiated discus-sion of it and, by influencing public opinion, established the climate of bigotry and misrepresentation which was to dominate attitudes in the first half of this century. Their decision to give lesbianism 'a scientific descrip-tion'[10] had the effect of imprisoning definitions of it firmly within male parameters. Both Havelock Ellis's representation of it as a congenital inversion and Freud's contrary view of it as an acquired orientation, one which represents, in his opinon, an immature stage of development, served to perpetuate existing prejudices, while also promoting new ones. By confusing lesbianism with masculinity, the two constructed a stereotype of the lesbian as unnaturally 'mannish'. They also helped to establish relationships with men as the only acceptable option for women, in this way re-enforcing the code of compulsory heterosexuality.

This negative interpretation of Freud and his influence has to be balanced, of course, by an acknowledgement of the positive aspects of his thought and the potential which it contains for a radical analysis of sexuality and desire. The latter is illustrated by the emphasis which he places on the contradictions of the unconscious and by his belief in the constructed nature of sexuality. However, it has taken the Lacanian revisions of Freudian thought and the reworking of Lacan by theorists with a feminist and/or gay perspective, such as Luce Irigaray,[11] John Fletcher[12] and Diane Hamer,[13] to uncover and develop the liberating aspect of these ideas. In the first half of the century they remained, on the whole, unrecognized. As far as women living in the period were concerned, it was the repressive aspects of Freudian theory which were visible. This explains why early members of the Lesbian Feminist Movement, such as Kate Millett[14] and Phyllis Chesler,[15] cast Freud in the role of 'the enemy', treating his name as a synonym for misogyny and lesbophobia.

As well as challenging the stereotype of the lesbian as 'mannish' and interested only in sex, the Lesbian Feminist Movement also reacted against the lesbian culture of the 1950s and 1960s and its approach to sex and gender. Lesbian feminists tend to regard butch-femme role-play in a negative light. They criticize it for imitating and reproducing heterosexual models of dominance and submission in sexual relations.[16] During the past decade attempts have been made to re-evaluate and valorize the practice. Its significance in the 1990s is, as we shall see, a controversial issue.

The closeted way of life which the majority of women who identified as lesbian in the first half of this century regarded as the norm has also generated debate. Although the subterfuge and secrecy which it involved could give rise to stress and feelings of alienation, they none the less held attractions by evoking the allure of the illicit.[17] Some women, far from welcoming the advent of the Lesbian Feminist Movement, appear to have resented its call to Come Out. They regretted the demise of the close-knit ties and 'secret agent' atmosphere of the old-style social life centering on a network of bars and clubs. One of them complains that, 'in this new world [of lesbian feminism] it seems like we're losing touch with the best of what we had: our tribes, our lesbian nation, our partisan underground.'[18]

The 'new world' created by the Lesbian Feminist Movement was to bring about major changes in attitude towards lesbianism and women's expectations of what a lesbian identification implies. Their revolutionary nature will become apparent in the following pages. The perspectives produced in the past twenty years, in the wake of the Movement, though certainly varied, are by no means random. They reflect, on the whole, two contrary approaches.

The first approach is political in emphasis and specifically feminist. By defining lesbianism in terms of woman-identification, it seeks to place it in a frame of feminist thought. In keeping with this, it defines lesbian relationships from the viewpoint of feminist camaraderie and woman bonding, and aims to establish connections between lesbian and heterosexual feminists.

The second approach which emerged in the mid-1980s, though encompassing different influences and points of view, may be generally described as 'libertarian'. The lesbian sexual radicals[19] who support it seek to challenge and supplant many of the ideas promulgated by the Lesbian Feminist Movement. Accusing lesbian feminists of attempting to desexualize lesbianism and 'sanitize' female sexuality by encouraging women to conform to a politically correct standard, they foreground the importance of sexual practice and a lesbian erotics. Instead of defining lesbian sexual attraction in terms of 'identification', they see 'difference' as the motivating impulse of desire. They also question the idealized representation of lesbian relationships, which some cultural feminists promoted, as untainted by conflict and power-struggle.[20] Social-constructionist theory and the increasing recognition of differences of race, class and ideological beliefs between women have also generated new attitudes.[21] Women influenced by them question the concept of a unitary lesbian identity and a homogeneous lesbian community and culture. Some of them, by participating in Queer Politics and forging alliances with gay men, also challenge the concepts of 'separatism' and 'women's space'. These are integral to lesbian feminist thought and, prior to the 1980s, were seldom questioned.

Another challenge to lesbian feminism has come from the poststructuralist thought of the academy. In some contemporary theoretical works the lesbian is seen less as an individual with a voice and identity than as a subject position created by the text. Emphasis is placed on the disruptive effect which lesbianism has on heterosexual culture and the binary gender code which characterizes it.[22]

The development of lesbian theory over the past twenty years has revolved on the whole around these two contrary poles of 'woman identification' and 'lesbian libertarianism'. They give rise, as we shall see, to definitions of the sign *lesbian* and assumptions about the lesbian way of life which are radically different.

Politics and woman-identification

A major obstacle confronting theorists writing in the 1970s in attempting to re-evaluate the sign *lesbian* and make connections between lesbianism and

feminism was the allegation that the lesbian is 'mannish' and, as Radicalesbians put it in 'The Woman Identified Woman', 'not a real woman'.[23]
Radicalesbians combat this charge with a strategy which is strikingly simple. Inverting the stereotype of the 'mannish' lesbian, they portray her,
instead, as the embodiment of true womanhood. Their line of argument, in
this respect, depends on the distinction which they make between the
woman who identifies as lesbian and the woman who identifies as heterosexual. The lesbian, they argue, in contrast to her heterosexual sisters who
achieve authenticity and status by identifying with men, is primarily committed to woman. Rejecting the patriarchal code of femininity which
relegates women to 'sexual and family functions' (p. 244), she acquires
identity and fulfilment from female relationships. In this way the concept of
woman–identification achieved prominence.[24] It was to become the hub of
lesbian feminist politics, dominating lesbian theory and holding its position
of centrality unchallenged until the 1980s.

'The Woman Identified Woman' also successfully demolishes another
commonplace misrepresentation. This is the notion, promoted by the sexologists, that lesbianism is to be defined by reference to particular sex acts.
Condemning society's propensity to lay 'a surrogate male role on the
lesbian' (p. 242) and regard her merely in terms of sex, Radicalesbians re-
define her as a signifier of feminist politics. The lesbian, they boldly an-
nounce in the opening paragraph of the essay, represents 'the rage of all
women condensed to the point of explosion' (p. 240). And, as well as
functioning as the archetypal feminist revolutionary, she also emerges as the
focal point of the feminist community. One of the most striking features of
'The Woman Identified Woman' is the way that, having acknowledged the
position of contempt and isolation to which homophobic society relegates
the lesbian, it goes on to portray her as the member of an integrated social
group. Addressing this topic, Radicalesbians write:

> Only women can give to each other a new sense of self. That identity
> we have to develop with reference to ourselves, and not in relation to
> men . . . For this we must be available and supportive to one another,
> give our commitment and our love, give the emotional support
> necessary to sustain this movement. Our energies must flow toward
> our sisters, not backward toward our oppressors. (p. 245)

This vivid evocation of lesbian community was, I remember, a source of
inspiration to many of us reading it in the 1970s. It encouraged us to work
to consolidate the fragile network of activist groups, help–lines and social
caucuses which we were in the process of creating and invest our energies
in communal projects. The picture of cooperation and group interaction
which it paints is totally at odds with the loneliness and alienation which,
having been taught by contemporary culture to regard ourselves as sick and
deviant, we had come to see as the norm of lesbian experience. The

concept of lesbian community was, in the 1970s, an innovative one. Though open to criticism on the grounds that it is over–idealistic and ignores racial and social differences between women, it is, in fact, from a political point of view, one of the most original and enabling ideas produced by the Lesbian Feminist Movement.[25]

'The Woman Identified Woman' is an important text not only in the respect that it is one of the earliest documents of the Lesbian Feminist Movement but also because it introduces in embryo many key ideas which subsequent theorists were to develop more fully. The concept of woman-identification receives analysis in Adrienne Rich's 'Compulsory Heterosexuality and Lesbian Existence' (1980),[26] while the significance of lesbian community is elaborated by Jill Johnston[27] and other writers.[28] The idea of lesbian separatism is taken to extreme lengths by the American Political Lesbian Movement[29] and the Leeds Revolutionary Feminist Group.[30] Meanwhile Charlotte Bunch[31] and Monique Wittig develop in different ways the lesbian critique of heterosexual values and institutions. Wittig questions and attempts to re-define the categories 'man' and 'woman'. She seeks, by challenging heterosexual systems of thought, to 'accomplish the destruction of heterosexuality as a social system which is based on the oppression of women by men'.[32]

Politically vigorous though 'The Woman Identified Woman' is, some of the arguments which it employs appear from the more complex perspective of present-day lesbian theory questionable and faulty. The representation of lesbianism as the signifier of feminism, which is the essay's key point, depends on the dubious and sleight-of-hand conflation of lesbian sexual and emotional relationships with women, with the political phenomena of feminist commitment and camaraderie. The critic objects that, although these impulses sometimes co-exist in a single individual, they do not always do so – and, anyway, they are not the same thing. The equation of lesbianism with feminist politics, which Radicalesbians helped to initiate, has proved in the long run problematic, since it has resulted in its sexual aspect being ignored or devalued. As Ann Snitow and her co-authors observe, 'In pointing to anger rather than eros as the wellspring of lesbianism, the manifesto opened the way for the desexualization of lesbian identity.'[33] This consequence was unintentional for, as they admit, 'How could theorists foresee that they could completely unsex an identity that had been all sex just a short time before?' (Snitow et al. 1984: 26) The truth is, the political theorization of lesbianism promoted by 'The Woman Identified Woman' and other similar essays turned out to be, ironically, too successful for its own good. Like many other works of political theory, the essay gave rise to effects which its authors, writing at an earlier moment of history and in a different intellectual context, were unable to foresee.

Another feature of 'The Woman Identified Woman' which strikes the present-day reader as problematic is that, in order to emphasize the strength and unity of the lesbian community, Radicalesbians portray women who identify as lesbian as a homogeneous group. They ignore the fact that, while some lesbians are staunch feminists and support the aims of the Lesbian Feminist Movement, others do not. However, regarded in the context of the disunity which existed among lesbians in the early 1970s, this strategy is not a problem but, on the contrary, a strength. As Zimmerman observes, 'Since heterosexist societies render lesbians invisible and unspeakable, to show and name large numbers and varieties of women as "lesbians" can be a political act . . . Such notions – often labelled essentialist – were important to the pioneering generation of the 1970s, and may still be of considerable consciousness–raising value today.'[34]

A more serious flaw in the essay is its confused and contradictory treatment of the positions, *vis à vis* feminism, of women who identify as lesbian and those who identify as heterosexual. The gist of its argument as a whole is to minimize the difference between the two categories by portraying the lesbian as the signifier of womanhood in general. She represents 'the rage of *all* women condensed to the point of explosion' (p. 240, italics added), and the reader has the impression that in the utopian future which Radicalesbians envisage 'Any woman', as the slogan states, 'can be lesbian'. However, these propositions rest, paradoxically, on the assertion of a moral distinction between lesbian and heterosexual women. While the former are celebrated for achieving independence and woman–identification, the latter are portrayed very negatively. They are represented as submitting passively to male domination and failing to give support to members of their own sex. As is often the case in the lesbian writing of the 1970s, fiction as well as theory, women who identify as heterosexual are made to appear unconvincingly passive figures totally controlled by men – a sort of lesbian feminist version of the robotic Stepford Wives!

Radicalesbians' unsatisfactory and simplistic treatment of the differences between lesbians and heterosexual women, and of sexuality in general, stems partly from the strategy of inversion on which they structure their essay. By inverting the stereotype of the lesbian as evil and depraved, they become locked in a system of binary opposites which leads them to portray lesbianism as wholly 'good' and heterosexuality as wholly 'bad'.[35] It also reflects, of course, the intellectual defects and limitations of the period. In the North America of the 1970s there was, in fact, no satisfactory model of female sexuality available for lesbian theorists to employ. Due to the conservative interpretation of Freudian theory current at the time, and the emphasis placed on a particularly narrow and conformist version of ego psychology, the majority of lesbians and feminists understandably rejected psychoanalytic theory as bigoted and misogynistic. Lacan's revision of Freudian thought was unfamiliar to the American public, while the analysis of femininity carried out by French feminist theorists such as Irigaray and Julia Kristeva had not yet been written or translated. As a result,

Radicalesbians are forced to rely on a conditioning model of sexuality.[36] This entraps them, despite the valiant attempts which they make to resist it and depict lesbianism as a construct, in an essentialist position. Female heterosexuality is condemned as a form of 'false consciousness' while lesbianism, in contrast, is celebrated as the 'true' female sexual identity. It is envisaged as a kind of core self, which in many women is repressed and waits, like the Sleeping Beauty in her enchanted palace, to be awoken and brought to light by the kiss of a lesbian Princess Charming.

A strand of thought in 'The Woman Identified Woman' which was to prove particularly influential in shaping lesbian feminist politics, and thus merits attention here, is a commitment to separatism. The demand that 'Our energies must flow towards our sisters, not backward toward our oppressors' (Radicalesbian 1973: 245) was to become a guiding principle in many women's lives. It was also, as the decade progressed, to prove increasingly controversial and problematic.

The separatist position advocated by Radicalesbians and other lesbian feminist theorists, though often criticized today as narrow and impractical, is in many respects positive and enabling. Without it, neither the Women's Liberation Movement nor the Lesbian Feminist Movement would have achieved the physical and psychological space necessary to organize and develop a sexual politics. However, while separatism can be a source of strength, when taken to extremes, as it was in the 1970s by the American Political Lesbian Movement and the British Leeds Revolutionary Feminist Group,[37] it can become a source of conflict and division. The demand voiced by these groups that women who identify as feminist cease to relate to men and become either lesbian or celibate, angered and alienated many women, lesbian as well as heterosexual. It was at this point, when the conflict between opposing factions was at its most destructive, that Rich intervened with the publication of her essay 'Compulsory Heterosexuality and Lesbian Existence'. The theory of lesbian continuum which it articulates, though problematic intellectually, is politically empowering and helped to heal these rifts.

Rich opens her essay by defining heterosexuality as an institution and listing the various strategies (sexual, social and economic) which patriarchal culture employs to recruit women into heterosexual relations. She goes on to describe lesbianism as a form of resistance to male power and introduces the term 'lesbian continuum', defining it as follows:

> I mean the term *lesbian continuum* to include a range – through each
> woman's life and throughout history – of woman-identified experi-
> ence, not simply the fact that a woman has had or consciously desired
> genital sexual experience with another woman. If we expand it to

embrace many more forms of primary intensity between and among women, including the sharing of a rich inner life, the bonding against male tyranny, the giving and receiving of practical and political support . . . we begin to grasp breadths of female history and psychology which have lain out of reach as a consequence of limited, mostly clinical definitions of *lesbianism*.[38]

As Rich points out, she deliberately uses the term 'lesbian continuum', as opposed to 'lesbian', to avoid the clinical and narrowly sexual associations of the latter. She seeks to signify by it ideas of female friendship and political comradeship, as well as sexual involvements between women.

The theory of lesbian continuum has met with a mixed response. Some commentators praise it for highlighting the multifaceted nature of female relationships and healing divisions between lesbian and heterosexual feminists by focusing attention on their common goals and interests. Jacquelyn N. Zita, whose views I endorse, welcomes Rich's definition of 'lesbianism as it exists under patriarchy as a part of a politics of woman-centered resistance'.[39]

However, the theory has also encountered criticism. Some argue that, by placing experiences of woman-bonding and feminist camaraderie on the lesbian continuum, Rich ignores or undervalues the sexual aspect of lesbianism. Elizabeth Wilson accuses her argument of being reductionist in the respect that it conflates the terms 'lesbian', 'feminist' and 'female', failing to distinguish between them.[40] Tania Modleski suggests that Rich carries the lesbian feminist propensity to represent lesbianism as the signifier of true womanhood, while underplaying its sexual component, to its logical conclusion. She claims that Rich 'allows the category of gender to overwhelm that of sexuality and ends by placing all women (insofar as they have friendships with other women) on the lesbian continuum', with the result that 'every woman is thus more or less lesbian'.[41]

Wilson's and Modleski's criticisms, though valid in some respects, strike me as imperceptive. As well as failing to relate Rich's theory sufficiently closely to the conflicts and disagreements between Political Lesbians and heterosexual feminists which form its context, they also do not appreciate the subtle distinctions and 'the sense of range and gradation'[42] which she brings to the definition of lesbian continuum. Rather than conflating the terms lesbian, feminist and female, as they accuse her of doing, she refers to 'a *range* of woman-identified experience' (my italics), which includes a variety of different forms of female attachments and sexual identifications. Inidcative of this range is the attraction which the theory of lesbian continuum holds for women of different sexual orientations. A member of the newly formed Bisexual Movement, it is interesting to note, admits to finding it enabling and gives a new and thought-provoking reading of it.[43]

Another facet of Rich's ideas which merits comment is her representation of the female subject's discovery of her lesbian orientation as 'a journey back to the mother'.[44] Like the object-relations theorist Nancy Chodorow, Rich concentrates attention on the fact that in phallocentric culture, while both sexes are expected to break their initial bond with the mother, the boy is allowed to reproduce facets of it in a displaced form in his subsequent relations with women whereas the girl, if she accommodates to heterosexuality, is not. She has to renounce intimate relationships with women altogether. Chodorow fails to relate these observations to the situation of the lesbian but both Rich and the British theorist Joanna Ryan develop them in this direction. Ryan argues that the analysis of lesbian relationships in the light of the pre-oedipal bond between mother and daughter is of major importance to the understanding of their emotional complexities and ambiguities.[45]

The notion that lesbian attachments may reproduce, in a displaced form, certain aspects of the involvement between mother and daughter is an intriguing proposition. Its weakness, as propounded by some theorists at any rate, lies in the fact that not only does it ignore the existence of male homosexuality but it may also be utilized by homophobes to argue that sexual relations between men are inexplicable and abnormal. As Diana Fuss wryly comments, it implies that 'heterosexuality is as natural and beneficial for men, as it is unnatural and destructive for women.'[46] This attitude, combined with the conventionally separatist position which she adopts, helps to explain Rich's prejudiced attitude towards male homosexuals. Uncritically reproducing homophobic stereotypes, she associates them with promiscuity and ageism (Rich, 1980: 53).

As the texts discussed above illustrate, the woman-identified approach to lesbianism interweaves a number of different strands – radical feminist, cultural feminist and psychoanalytic. Another strand in its composition is exemplified by the work of African-American theorists. As early as 1957 a letter by the dramatist Lorraine Hansberry published in *The Ladder*, an American lesbian periodical, affirms the connection between lesbianism and feminism, by drawing attention to the links between anti-feminism and lesbophobia.[47] A writer who develops these ideas and articulates a woman-identified point of view is Audre Lorde. In an essay published in 1978 she describes the erotic as 'a resource within each of us that lies in a deeply female and spiritual plane'.[48] She argues that men, fearing its empowering effect on women, seek to appropriate and trivialize it by conflating it with the pornographic. Like Rich, whose cultural feminist perspective she shares, Lorde brings together dimensions which patriarchal culture regards as separate, by linking the spiritual and the emotional with the political. Refusing to limit the erotic to the specifically sexual, she describes it as achieving expression in 'the sharing of joy, whether physical, emotional, psychic or intellectual' (Lorde 1984: 56). She concludes the essay by encouraging women who, like herself, accept a woman-identified perspective, to recognize and acknowledge its power. In this way, she claims, they will achieve the energy to bring about political and social change.

Certain theorists who work within a poststructuralist frame also regard lesbianism from a political perspective. Irigaray, writing in a psychoanalytic context, describes lesbianism as representing an alternative sexual economy to the phallocentric model endorsed by the dominant culture. Discussing the role of object of exchange which women are expected to play, she recommends that they reject and elude it by refusing to relate to men and forming attachments with one another.[49] She criticizes Freud for misrepresenting lesbianism by explaining it in terms of a 'masculinity complex', and regards his failure to recognize the importance of lesbian pleasure as symptomatic of society's lack of understanding of female pleasure in general and its misogynistic propensity to define it within male parameters (Irigaray, *This Sex Which is Not One,* pp. 42–4; 193–7). Irigaray argues that the lesbian, by means of her very existence, exposes the contradictions in heterosexual models of femininity and reveals the control which phallocentric systems of thought exert upon women. The lesbian, as a commentator explains,

> exposes 'mature femininity' (*Speculum,* p. 112, citing Freud) as, in effect, mere masquerade, imposed on women by men. By desiring another woman 'like a man', the lesbian mimics and plays with the masculinity and femininity of psychoanalytic discourse, thereby making both 'visible' as constructions and performances. At the same time she discovers, creates, 'what an exhilerating pleasure it is to be partnered with someone like herself' (*Speculum,* p. 103). For Irigaray, then, the lesbian demonstrates that women 'are not simply reabsorbed' by a male-defined femininity: '*They also remain elsewhere* . . .' (*Ce Sexe,* p. 76).[50]

Irigaray, while highlighting the subversive role which the lesbian plays in revealing the flaws and contradictions in phallocentric concepts of femininity, certainly cannot be accused of representing lesbian relationships in an idealized light. In discussing the effects of *déréliction,* the state of hopelessness and alienation to which she believes women to be relegated on account of the fact that the mother/daughter relationship is unsymbolized, she draws attention to the problematic aspect of female attachments and groupings, both lesbian and heterosexual.[51] In *L'Ethique de la Différence Sexuelle* (1984) she includes in her account of the difficulties to which lesbian involvements are prone 'confusions of identity' and 'non-perception of difference'.[52]

In contrast to Irigaray, though sharing with her an emphasis on the political significance of lesbianism and its destabilizing effect on the gender-constructs of the dominant culture, is Monique Wittig, who refuses to associate lesbianism with a female/feminine economy. In taking this line, Wittig also differs from the other theorists discussed in this section. Influenced by the perspectives of the Lesbian Feminist Movement, they all base their theorization of lesbianism on the concept of woman-identification. Wittig, on the contrary, unexpectedly asserts that 'lesbians are not women', and that the concept lesbian 'is beyond the category of sex'.[53] This is, in fact, not as bizarre as it at first appears. Wittig aligns the sign *lesbian* with neither masculinity nor femininity, but employs it to expose the artifice of the division between the two and to problematize the categories of sex and gender as defined by heterosexual culture.

Wittig's decision to dissociate the lesbian from the sign *woman* is motivated not by the homophobic intent of pathologizing lesbianism, as was the case with the male sexologists, but by the desire to highlight the lesbian's rejection of, and independence from, the conventional feminine role and position. The terms *man/woman*, Wittig points out, exist in binary opposition, with *woman* functioning as inferior and subordinate. By rejecting a relationship with a man, the lesbian both eludes the category *woman* and exposes the fact that it is a cultural construct. In Wittig's view, 'What makes a woman is a specific social relation to a man . . . a relation which lesbians escape by refusing to become or stay heterosexual' (Wittig 1992: 20).

The contradictions in Wittig's theorization of lesbianism intrigue contemporary theorists. With the possible exception of Rich's 'Compulsory Heterosexuality and Lesbian Existence', her essays have received more exegesis and analysis than any other lesbian theoretical works before or since! Critics point out that, while Wittig's representation of the concept *lesbian* as destabilizing the binary gender system of the dominant culture anticipates a poststructuralist approach, she falls into the trap of essentialism, by depicting lesbians as a homogeneous group with a unitary politics and ideology. She also creates an idealized image of lesbian culture by describing it as a 'free space' untainted by heterosexual values and power-relations.[54]

However, despite the flaws and inconsistencies which it reveals, Wittig's theorization of lesbianism is politically empowering. It portrays the lesbian as a disruptive influence who subversively exposes the gaps and contradictions in heterosexual structures and systems of thought. This is an important role. It is one which, as we shall see in subsequent chapters, writers of fiction, as well as theory, often assign to her.

Libertarian and poststructuralist approaches

The 1980s was a turbulent period for lesbian politics. Women who identified as lesbian witnessed the emergence of certain very different attitudes and perspectives from those of the previous decade. A distinctive feature of this new approach was that, in contrast to Lesbian Feminism which theorizes lesbianism from the viewpoint of woman-identification, it foregrounds the importance of sex and the erotic. And, unlike lesbian feminists who tend to regard relationships between women in terms of similarity, assuming both partners to be woman-identified and to adopt a similarly androgynous image, the lesbian sexual radicals see them in terms of 'difference'. Emphasis is placed on the dominant/submissive roles of butch-femme identification or, in a minority of cases, a sado-masochistic (SM) partnership. Difference, rather than identification, is regarded as the pivot of desire.[55]

Another characteristic of the libertarian approach is the rejection of an emphasis on separatism in favour of a focus on lesbians and gay men working and socializing together. The willingness of lesbians to mix with gay men, as well as reflecting a desire to participate in the fight against AIDS, stems from a recognition of common interests.[56] The homophobic backlash, exemplified in the United Kingdom by the introduction of Section 28[57] and in North America by certain anti-gay measures and laws,[58] is directed at lesbians as well as male homosexuals. An interest in sex provides another link between the two groups. Rather than criticizing gay men for their chauvinism and promiscuity and complaining that they dominate clubs and social events, as some lesbian feminists do, the lesbian sexual radicals, as is illustrated by an episode in DeLynn's *Don Juan in the Village* (1990),[59] are likely to express envy and admiration at their adventurous approach to sex.

The effect which these ideas have had on the lesbian population as a whole is difficult to assess. In my experience, few women subscribe wholly to a libertarian position. The majority of us, particularly women over the age of 40, continue to see lesbianism from the viewpoint of woman-identification and to relate it, in general terms at least, to feminism. However, this does not mean that we are uninfluenced by libertarian attitudes. In the past few years the lesbian community has concerned itself notably less with the issue of 'political correctness'. A greater degree of tolerance is apparent, with bisexuals and married women more generally accepted at social events. This coexists with a greater diversity of attitudes to sex roles and dress. Moreover, as Faderman illustrates,[60] unemployment, combined with the increase in public expressions of homophobia, have generated a new spirit of compromise in values and lifestyle. Whereas in the 1970s the lesbian who expressed an interest in pursuing a professional career or achieving material security by buying a house was sometimes criticized as male-identified or 'bourgeois', in the 1990s her plans are likely to meet with acceptance.

While the origins of the libertarian approach to lesbianism are too complex to discuss here, a key event in their emergence was the attempt in the early 1980s to introduce the discussion of sexuality onto the feminist agenda. This was not limited to lesbians but reflected a feeling of dissatisfaction among women in general at the failure of the Women's Movement to address the topic of sexuality. The preoccupation with sex and desire which characterized this period was motivated partly by the growing interest in feminist psychoanalysis, a discourse which, as the decade progressed, was to become increasingly influential. The publication of studies by British and American women working in the field, such as Juliet Mitchell,[61] Jacqueline Rose[62] and Jessica Benjamin,[63] and the increasing availability of translated versions of the work of the French feminist theorists Hélène Cixous, Irigaray and Kristeva, meant that, though some die-hard radical feminists continued to maintain an attitude of hostility towards it, psychoanalysis could no longer simply be dismissed as 'the enemy'. On the contrary, as many of us recognized, it offers valuable tools for analysing sexuality and gender. We felt that not only had the Movement failed to take advantage of these but also that certain sections of it, by promoting censorship and repressive attitudes, were deliberately blocking the discussion of sex. A comment voiced by the contributors to the British Journal *Feminist Review* (Summer 1985) epitomizes these sentiments: 'We feel that the Women's Movement has become more concerned with constructing and policing its own categories of sexual identity than with attempting to understand the complex and often contradictory construction of women's sexuality in a male-dominated, capitalist society.'[64] Complaints of a similar kind were expressed by American theorists and writers. Benjamin criticizes the Movement for trying to 'sanitize or rationalize the erotic, fantastic components of human life', and accuses it of responding to female fantasies of domination 'with moral condemnation rather than understanding'.[65] Joan Nestle, describing the difficulties which she experienced in finding a publisher for an essay she had written on butch-femme role-play, graphically portrays herself as trapped between 'the Lesbian-feminist antipornography movement on the one side, and the homophobic and antisex mentality of some straight people on the other'.[66] She complains that a hierarchy of respectability operates in the lesbian community, and protests at the accusations of political incorrectness directed at 'leather and butch and femme Lesbians, transsexuals, Lesbian prostitutes and sex workers, writers of explicit sexual stories . . .' (Nestle 1987: 149).

Two national conferences were instrumental in challenging these repressive attitudes. The feminist conference held at Barnard University, New York City, in 1982, and the lesbian one held in London in 1983 focused particular attention on the discussion of sexuality.[67] Both included workshops and papers on sexual fantasy and unorthodox forms of sexual practice, such as sadomasochism and butch-femme identification.

Collections of essays which bring together lesbian and heterosexual perspectives on sex, such as *Desire: The Politics of Sexuality* (Snitow *et al.* 1984) and the 1981 edition of the American journal *Heresies* (12, vol. 3, no. 4), also helped to promote a libertarian viewpoint. Commenting on the differences between old and new attitudes to lesbianism which they reflect, Susan Ardill and Sue O'Sullivan observe, 'Whereas the British revolutionary feminists appeared to see sex as a pleasant possibility between women who had withdrawn from men, *Sex Heresies* underlined the deep and confusing currents of desire between women.'[68]

Although the essays championing the new libertarian approach, such as those in *Heresies* and the SAMOIS collection *Coming to Power* (1981), make provocative reading, many of them are intellectually disappointing, since they lack rigour and depth. Benjamin, pinpointing their defects, accuses the defenders of SM of treating the topic superficially and failing to analyse its psychological significance. They are content, she complains, merely to describe women's sexual fantasies but show little interest in discussing 'what such fantasies mean and why they hold such power over our imagination'.[69] Her criticism is, in my view, just. Much of the writing produced by the lesbian sexual radicals appears to be motivated less by the aim of genuinely exploring a lesbian erotics than by an urge to demolish lesbian feminist ideals and shock the reader. By simply inverting the political, woman-identified view of lesbianism adopted by their predecessors, they perpetuate the phallocentric system of binaries and, more often than not, become locked in a set of attitudes which are similarly dogmatic and one-sided. Their perspective strikes the reader, in some ways, as not radical at all but downright *old-fashioned*. It revives the simplistic identification of lesbianism with sex, which the Lesbian Feminist Movement successfully challenged. Moreover, in seeking to oppose so-called 'feminist moralism', it runs the risk of reducing sex to the level of experimentation and a form of consumerism, in which practices of all kinds (including paedophilia and prostitution) are equally acceptable.[70]

Libertarian accounts of lesbianism frequently focus on two particular forms of sexual practice – sadomasochism and butch-femme identification. Both reflect positions of dominance/submission and thus challenge the idealistic view, promoted by some lesbian feminists, of lesbian partnerships as untainted by inequality or power-struggle.

That it should be SM, a marginal sexual practice which is arguably of interest to only a small minority of women, which has come to assume a position of centrality in the lesbian 'Sex Wars',[71] acting as the signifier of the libertarian approach to lesbianism in general, is, as commentators agree, surprising. Explanations for the importance assigned to it differ. Some theorists argue that SM epitomizes 'the most vital components of *all* erotic tension: teasing, titillation, compulsion and denial, control and struggle, pleasure and pain',[72] while simultaneously providing an arena for sexual play. An alternative explanation is that it 'makes possible the enactment of power fantasies in a safe situation', and symbolizes 'sexual outlawry and the dark side of self and forbidden desires'.[73] It thus undermines the lesbian feminist attempt to sanitize desire and sexual practice by rendering them politically correct. As Elizabeth Wilson, the author of this hypothesis, suggests, 'Perhaps feminism really has done something to lesbianism in

confusing it with non-eroticized love between women, so that some lesbians have been attracted to other, more deeply "forbidden" ways of
insisting that lesbianism *is* about sex' (Wilson 1983: 38).

However, when we turn to the texts produced by the advocates of SM,
such as those contained in the SAMOIS collection *Coming to Power*, we find
that the approach which they employ does not match up to Wilson's
interpretation. The contributors display an unexpected propensity to nor-
malize SM practice and, as Modleski humorously remarks, to 'minimize the
issues of power and violence that one would have thought to be definitely
inherent in sado-masochistic practices, ultimately implying that whips,
razors, and nipple clips are part of the panoply of devices to be used in
furthering the practices of "laudable humanistic virtues"'.[74] Susan Farr, a
member of the SAMOIS group, opens 'The Art of Discipline' by favour-
ably contrasting the consensual infliction of pain, which occurs in SM, with
the indiscriminate acts of violence, such as rape, battery and war, which
characterize patriarchal society. Emphasizing the element of playacting
which SM involves, she draws attention to the exchange of roles which
takes place between the two partners, cheerfully reminding the reader that
'the vulnerable submissive of today is the firm and strict dominant of
tomorrow'.[75] Passages such as this have the effect of muting the element of
dominance/subordination, and transforming the SM encounter into a
transaction which is almost egalitarian. Farr also argues that SM is therapeutic; she claims that it enables herself and her partner to work out in a safe
and controlled situation the conflicts and tensions in their relationship.

The arguments employed by the advocates of SM are highly subjective –
and opponents of it, exemplified by members of the group Feminists
Against SM, counter them with ones which are similarly subjective. Both
sides tend to exaggerate the importance of the practice and, by universalizing its significance, credit it with an influence quite out of proportion to
that which it actually has. Defenders of SM, emphasizing its consensual
aspect, celebrate it as therapeutic, while Feminists Against SM respond by
condemning it as a major source of oppression. While the former insist that
SM practice appeals to fantasy and is unrelated to 'real life', the latter reply
by equating it with misogyny and racism.[76]

Racist attitudes certainly do inform some SM writing, as Samira M.
Kawash demonstrates in a cogently argued essay. Unlike other critics of SM
who concentrate on attacking its superficial features such as the imagery of
whips and bondage and the references to the roles of master and slave,
Kawash examines the way the concept of racial otherness is employed as a
frame for the free play of sexual possibilities and the break-down of the
categories of sex and gender which the SM encounter seeks to achieve. She
argues convincingly that 'It appears that [in contemporary racist society]
the very possibility of a sexual space apart depends on a rhetoric of race,
difference and otherness.'[77]

Another problematic feature of SM is the tendency of its advocates and practitioners to make an absolute distinction between SM sex and the so-called 'vanilla' variety, and to ignore the element of interplay which exists between the two. Some of the most intelligent discussions, it is interesting to note, come not from women who are personally involved in SM but from theorists who seek to explore its psychoanalytic implications. Modleski, for example, interprets one of the scenarios depicted in *Coming to Power* by reference to the figure of the symbolic mother. She makes the interesting suggestion that in lesbian SM 'what is being mocked and beaten out of the woman is . . . most accurately described as the law of gender itself, in its patriarchal form.'[78]

Butch–femme identification, another topic which the libertarian approach to lesbianism has brought to the fore, has also generated debate. The lesbian sexual radicals, challenging those women who criticize the practice for reproducing the inequalities of heterosexual relationships, attempt to re-interpret it in a positive light. Nestle, looking back nostalgically on the lesbian social scene of the 1950s and 1960s, celebrates butch–femme relations as 'an erotic partnership serving both as a conspicuous flag of rebellion and as an intimate exploration of women's sexuality'.[79] She defends the butch–identified woman from the charge of mimicking the male role and praises her courage for assuming responsibility in sexual enounters (Nestle 1987: 100). She also rejects the view of the femme role as an artificial construct but claims that, in adopting it, she 'did what was natural to me' (p. 103).

Nestle's affirmative account of butch–femme identification conflicts with that of other women who participated in the lesbian scene in the 1950s and 1960s. Many American and British lesbians, while acknowledging the practical function which role-play performed in making lesbians socially visible and providing a structure for their relationships in a homophobic era, argue that these advantages were achieved at a high price. They concentrate attention not only on the independence and status which the butch role conferred but also on the chauvinistic attitudes and sexual inhibitions which it fostered. Their evaluation of the femme role is similarly ambiguous. They point out that, while it gave women the licence to express emotional vulnerability, dress up, and rely on their butch partners for protection, it simultaneously made them subordinate socially.[80] Elizabeth Wilson records that in the London of the 1960s the woman typecast as femme was treated as 'the lowest of the low'.[81]

As theorists are starting to perceive, not only are the positions and roles which lesbians adopt in their relations with one another very complex, but they are also subject to conflicting social and psychological interpretations. Whereas some women regard positions of dominance/submission in essentialist terms as 'innate', others see them as influenced by psychological and cultural factors. Still others regard them in a voluntaristic light, in terms of choice and personal preference; they foreground the subject's ability to play with and parody concepts of gender, by shifting from role to role at will. In this latter postmodern reading, one which is popular with some young lesbians, the partners adopt and switch roles consciously, regarding them in terms of 'performance'.[82] As Chapter 6 illustrates, these three different perspectives influence the treatment of lesbian partnerships in novels and stories. Fictional representations are, in fact, as varied as their theoretical counterparts.

By acknowledging the psychological complexity of female sexuality and promoting the analysis of different sexual identifications and positions, libertarian attitudes have also opened up a space for the discussion of *bisexuality*. This is a welcome step for, in the 1970s and early 1980s when lesbian feminist attitudes dominated lesbian thought, bisexuality was the subject of confusion and misunderstanding. The Lesbian Feminist Movement not only refused to recognize it as a valid option but also, in some cases, promoted a climate of hostility towards women who identified as bisexual.[83] Two stereotypes of the bisexual existed, both of which were pejorative and portrayed her as a disruptive influence. She was typecast either as weak and vacillating, easily seduced by men into betraying her lesbian comrades, or as exploitative and manipulative, taking advantage of their good will only to to desert them in times of crisis and take refuge in heterosexual privilege.[84] The emergence of these stereotypes, simplistic and unjust though they are, is understandable and, in the case of some women, they perhaps contain a grain of truth. The burgeoning lesbian groups of the early 1970s, as well as being experimental, were extremely fragile. Their survival depended on a strong act of commitment from their members. Heterosexist pressures posed a serious threat – and the ability to trust one's sisters was of paramount importance. In addition, the services of counsellors, therapists, group facilitators and all the other agencies to which individuals and groups can now turn for help were non-existent – in the provinces, at least. It was all we could do to cope with our own complex emotions without dealing with those of woman who, many of us felt, rightly or wrongly, had a stake in preserving the very hetero-patriarchy which we were intent on challenging.

Only recently, with the formation of bisexual groups and organizations,[85] have women who identify as bisexual had the opportunity to express their own viewpoint and rectify the misunderstandings and prejudices which they have suffered. *Closer to Home: Bisexuality and Feminism* (Weise 1992) illustrates their work in this area. The essays which it contains combine autobiographical anecdotes with theoretical analysis. The contributors, utilizing the ideas of Derrida and Cixous, argue that a bisexual lifestyle represents a challenge to the binary opposites and dualistic systems of thought which inform Western culture.[86] It also challenges the concept of a unitary, static sexual identity, along with the homosexual/heterosexual dichotomy, which underpin sexual relations in contemporary society (Weise 1992: 258, 385).

The writing of the lesbian sexual radicals, as well as promoting the discussion of different sexual identifications including bisexuality, has also influenced lesbian social and political allegiances. It has encouraged women to question the concept of separatism by forming social and political links with men. Some women who identify as lesbian have joined Queer Nation, a New York direct-action group formed in the late 1980s with the aim of responding to the AIDS crisis and stemming the tide of violence against lesbians and gays. The choice of the term 'Queer', as well as valorizing a word habitually used as a term of abuse, allows for a focus on different sexual identifications – bisexual, transsexual and heterosexual, as well as lesbian and gay. The various branches of Queer Nation, such as the American ACT UP and the British OutRage, disillusioned with conventional campaigning methods which involve working with the state, employ ones which are theatrical and more direct.[87] They stage kiss-ins, queer weddings, and other events involving performance and parody. The use which they make of direct action resembles the activities of the 1970s Women's Liberation Movement, which organized marches and examples of street-theatre to highlight issues of childcare, violence against women and reproductive rights.

The precise relationship which lesbians have to Queer Nation is open to question. Although women play a part in the events which it stages, many lesbians, myself included, are critical of its perspectives and agenda. We dislike the term 'queer', resent the excessive attention which a few 'star' figures asssociated with it receive in the media and press, and regard the public attacks which some of its members make on the Women's Movement as provocative and unjust.[88] As in the days of the 1970s Gay Liberation Front, complaints are voiced that men dominate the action and the choice of campaigning issues. Black lesbians and lesbians of colour feel especially marginalized. As one perceptively comments, 'The map of the new Queer Nation would have a male face and mine and those of many of my sisters of colour would be simply background material.'[89] Many black lesbians and gays, alienated and angered by the prevalence of racist attitudes, either form groups of their own or, choosing to put their energies into campaigns relating to race, join forces with heterosexuals from their own ethnic background and culture.

In summing up the changes which have occurred in approaches to lesbianism since the 1970s, one recognizes certain topics as assuming particular importance. A significant achievement of black and Asian lesbians has been to challenge the concept of a unitary lesbian identity and question the representation of lesbians as a single, homogeneous group.[90] In addition, the lesbian sexual radicals, by provoking the Women's Movement out of its silence on sex, have succeeded in countering the prescriptive attitudes towards sex roles and dress,[91] which existed in some, though not all, lesbian circles in the 1970s, and promoting the discussion of different positions and identifications.

The 1980s and 1990s have also witnessed the development of Lesbian and Gay Studies in colleges and universities. As a consequence, the influence of poststructuralist perspectives and modes of thought is increasingly apparent. An effect of this, as Zimmerman points out, is 'the deconstruction of the lesbian as a unified, essentialist, ontological being and the reconstruction of her as a metaphor and/or subject position'.[92] Concepts of this kind, though useful from the point of view of textual analysis and valuable in countering the notion of a unitary lesbian identity, run the risk of creating an esoteric, elite discourse which is intelligible only to an intellectual few. At the moment it is dominated by the work of a few brilliant thinkers, such as Butler and Fuss.

While disliking the esoteric tone and elitist attitudes associated with the new poststructuralist trend in Lesbian Studies, I find some of the questions which its exponents address productive and challenging. One important question which exercises the minds of theorists at present is, how do we define the relation and interaction between lesbianism and heterosexuality? Wittig's idealistic representation of lesbianism as occupying a privileged space which exists outside the hetero-patriarchal system has been challenged by Fuss, who argues that lesbian relations are inevitably implicated in heterosexual structures.[93] Butler and Sue-Ellen Case approach the question from a different point of view – the postmodern concept of gender as production and performance. Butler challenges the commonly held assumption that lesbian and gay identities, as exemplified by butch–femme and drag roles, are imitations or imperfect copies of 'natural' heterosexual originals. She argues that, on the contrary, the strategies of parodic reworking which they involve have the effect of exposing the constructed and imperfect aspect of the so-called 'originals'.[94] Case, basing her discussion on Joan Riviere's theory of the feminine masquerade and the interplay between masculine and feminine positions on which it is grounded, claims that the butch–femme couple enacts a performance which parodies and 'camps up' the phallic economy of the heterosexual partnership.[95]

Lesbian theory has made remarkable progress since its inception in the early 1970s. It has given rise to developments the diversity and complexity of which those of us who participated in discussion groups and consciousness-raising meetings in the early days of the Lesbian Movement certainly could not foresee. Its most attractive feature is its diversity – and it would be pleasant to conclude this chapter on an affirmative note by concentrating on its positive aspects. However, lesbian theory in the 1990s, despite its notable achievements, reveals certain problematic features which need to be acknowledged and addressed. For example, there is little sign that it has acquired the political maturity and breadth of vision necessary to combat the wave of homophobia which is currently making life intolerable for many British and American lesbians and gay men, and, by so doing, to help ameliorate their situation. On the contrary, as mentioned above, theorists (poststructuralist ones, in particular) frequently choose to work in areas which have little relevance to the majority of the gay community. This exacerbates the division between academic and popular approaches to lesbianism which, as I mentioned in Chapter 1, is a worrying feature of contemporary lesbian culture.

Another problematic aspect of contemporary lesbian theory is that all too often its apparent variety of perspective masks an underlying narrowness and rigidity. Theorists appear incapable of liberating themselves from the tyranny of the binary system and the antitheses of 'either/or'. A complaint voiced by Snitow and her co-authors in relation to feminist approaches to sex in general makes this point. They justly argue that 'We have gone from extreme to extreme. Instead of adding each new possibility to the list of gains, we have, rather, traded in the old for the new.' The consequence is, 'We oscillate between two perspectives: on the one hand, a self-righteous feminine censoriousness and, on the other, a somewhat cavalier libertarianism.'[96] This comment is relevant to the Lesbian Movement. In the past two decades we have swung to and fro between what we mistakenly see as the contraries of politics/sex, pleasure/political correctness, identification/difference, activism/academia. We find difficulty uniting these interests and the ideological positions which they represent. Lacking any real sense of lesbian history, we tend to repeat the same mistakes as our predecessors and fall into the same intellectual traps – often without recognizing the fact.[97]

This impasse is, of course, not entirely of our own making but reflects the dichotomies and rigid systems of thought which characterize the phallocentric culture in which we live. Finding strategies to liberate ourselves from it is not easy – and is a task for the theorists of the future.

Notes

1 Examples include Alice Echols, 'The New Feminism of Yin and Yang', in *Desire: The Politics of Sexuality*, ed. cit., pp. 62–81; Cora Kaplan's critique of Millett's thought in 'Radical Feminism and Literature: Rethinking Millett's *Sexual Politics*', in *Sea Changes: Essays on Culture and Feminism* (Verso, 1986), pp. 15–30; and Tania Modleski's critique of Rich's theory of lesbian continuum, in *Feminism Without Women: Culture and Criticism in a 'Postfeminist' Age* (Routledge, 1991), pp. 151–2.

2 Sue Cartledge and Susan Hemmings, 'How Did We Get This Way?', in Marsha Rowe (ed.) *Spare Rib Reader* (Penguin, 1982), p. 333.

3 This book is edited by Anne Koedt, Ellen Levine and Anita Rapone (Quadrangle).

4 For information about lines in the United Kingdom, phone London Lesbian Line, (071) 251 6911, Monday and Friday 2–10pm; Tuesday, Wednesday, Thursday 7–10pm. The Cambridge Line operates on (0223) 311753, Friday 7–10pm.

5 Zimmerman, *The Safe Sea of Women*, ed. cit., p. 97.

6 Edited by Sarah Julia Hoagland and Julia Penelope (Onlywomen).

7 See Anna Coote and Beatrix Campbell (eds) *Sweet Freedom: The Struggle for Women's Liberation* (Picador, 1982), pp. 31–5.

8 Anne Oakley and Juliet Mitchell (eds) *The Rights and Wrongs of Women* (Penguin, 1976), p. 12.

9 Edited by Christian McEwen and Sue O'Sullivan (Virago).

10 See Sheila Jeffreys, *The Spinster and Her Enemies: Feminism and Sexuality 1880–1930* (Pandora, 1985), p. 105; and Faderman, *Odd Girls and Twilight Lovers*, ed. cit., pp. 239–53.

11 See Margaret Whitford, *Luce Irigaray: Philosophy in the Feminine* (Routledge, 1991).

12 Fletcher, 'Freud and His Uses: Psychoanalysis and Gay Theory', in Simon Shepherd and Mick Wallis (eds) *Coming on Strong: Gay Politics and Culture* (Unwin Hyman, 1989), pp. 90–118.

13 Hamer, 'Significant Others', ed. cit., pp. 134–51.

14 Millet, *Sexual Politics* (Avon, 1971).

15 Chesler, *Women and Madness* (Doubleday, 1972).

16 Sheila Jeffreys, 'Butch and Femme: Now and Then', in Lesbian History Group (ed.) *Not a Passing Phase: Reclaiming Lesbians in History 1840–1985* (Women Press, 1989), pp. 158–87.

17 See Ann Snitow, Christine Stansell and Sharon Thompson (eds) *Desire: The Politics of Sexuality*, ed. cit., p. 22.

18 Quoted in Zimmerman, *The Safe Sea of Women*, ed. cit., p. 122.

19 Faderman, *Odd Girls and Twilight Lovers*, ed. cit., p. 252.

20 For reference to these ideas see Faderman, *Odd Girls and Twilight Lovers*, ed. cit., pp. 189–308; and Sedgwick, *Epistemology of the Closet*, pp. 34–9.

21 Zimmerman, 'Lesbians Like This and That', ed. cit., pp. 2–3.

22 For reference to the influence of poststructuralism on Lesbian Studies see the essays by Munt and Zimmerman in Munt (ed.) *New Lesbian Criticism*, ed. cit., ix–xxii, pp. 1–15; and Karla Jay and Joanne Glasgow (eds) *Lesbian Texts and Contexts: Radical Revisions* (New York University Press, 1990).

23 Radicalesbians, *Radical Feminism*, ed. cit., p. 242.

24 The history of 'woman-identification' is complex. Simone de Beauvoir touches on the concept in *The Second Sex* (1949), but it achieved full political definition in the 1970s. For reference to it see the entry 'Woman Identified Woman; in Cheris Kramarae and Paula A. Treichler, *A Feminist Dictionary* (Pandora, 1985), p. 494; and Zimmerman, *The Safe Sea of Women*, ed. cit., pp. 126–35.

25 Zimmerman, too, remarks on the originality of the concept of lesbian community. She points out that it originated in the early 1970s and that 'no idea of community can be found in the earliest examples of lesbian fiction (between roughly 1964 and 1973)' (*The Safe Sea of Women*, ed. cit., p. 129).

26 Rich, *Blood, Bread and Poetry: Selected Prose 1979–1985* (Virago, 1987), pp. 23–75.

27 Johnston, *Lesbian Nation: The Feminist Solution* (Simon and Schuster, 1974).

28 See Hoagland and Penelope, *For Lesbians Only*, ed. cit., pp. 41–55, 72–83.

29 CLIT Statement no. 2, in Hoagland and Penelope, *For Lesbians Only*, ed. cit., pp. 357–67. See also Coote and Campbell, op. cit., pp. 222–7.

30 Leeds Revolutionary Feminist Group, 'Political Lesbianism: The Case Against Heterosexuality' (1979), in Onlywomen Press (ed.) *Love Your Enemy? The Debate between Heterosexual Feminism and Political Lesbianism* (Onlywomen, 1981), pp. 5–10.

31 Bunch, 'Not for Lesbians Only', in Bunch and Gloria Steinem (eds) *Building Feminist Theory: Essays from Quest* (Longman, 1981), pp. 67–73.

32 Wittig, 'One is Not Born a Woman' (1981) in *The Straight Mind and Other Essays* (Harvester Wheatsheaf, 1992), p. 20.

33 Snitow, Stansell and Thompson, *Desire: The Politics of Sexuality*, ed. cit., p. 25.

34 Zimmerman, 'Lesbians Like This and That', ed. cit., p. 9.

35 Judith Butler's critique of the strategy of inversion (in *Gender Trouble: Feminism and the Subversion of Identity*, Routledge, 1990, pp. 26–7) is relevant to Radicalesbians' use of the strategy and the problems in which it involves them.

36 For reference to the conditioning model see Rosalind Coward, *Patriarchal Precedents: Sexuality and Social Relations* (Routledge and Kegan Paul, 1983), pp. 262–8.

37 See the essays cited in Notes 29 and 30. For reference to the concept of separatism see Zimmerman, *The Safe Sea of Women*, ed. cit., pp. 126–35.

38 Rich, 'Compulsory Heterosexuality and Lesbian Existence', ed. cit., pp. 51–2.

39 Zita, 'Historical Amnesia and the Lesbian Continuum', in Nannerl O. Keohane, Michelle Rosaldo and Barbara C. Gelpi (eds) *Feminist Theory: A Critique of Ideology* (Harvester, 1982), p. 170.

40 Wilson, 'I'll Climb the Stairway to Heaven: Lesbianism in the Seventies', in Sue Cartledge and Joanna Ryan (eds) *Sex and Love: New Thoughts on Old Contradictions* (Women's Press, 1983), pp. 187–9.

41 Modleski, *Feminism Without Women*, ed. cit., p. 151.

42 Snitow, Stansell and Thompson, the 'Afterword' to 'Compulsory Heterosexuality and Lesbian Continuum', in Rich, *Blood, Bread and Poetry*, ed. cit., p. 70.

43 See Rebecca Kaplan, 'Compulsory Heterosexuality and the Bisexual Existence: Toward a Bisexual Feminist Understanding of Heterosexism', in Elizabeth Reba Weise (ed.) *Closer to Home: Bisexuality and Feminism* (Seal Press, 1992), pp. 269–80.

44 Zimmerman, *The Safe Sea of Women*, ed. cit., p. 58.

45 Ryan, 'Psychoanalysis and Women Loving Women', in *Sex and Love*, ed. cit., pp. 196–209.

46 Fuss, *Essentially Speaking*, ed. cit., p. 48. Fuss also criticizes Monique Wittig for revealing a similar blind spot.

47 Reprinted in Gloria T. Hull, Patricia Bell Scott and Barbara Smith (eds) *All Women Are White, All the Blacks Are Men, But Some of Us Are Brave: Black Women's Studies* (Feminist Press, 1982), xxiii.

48 Lorde, 'Uses of the Erotic: The Erotic as Power', in *Sister Outsider: Essays and Speeches* (Crossing Press, 1984), p. 53.

49 Irigaray, *This Sex Which is Not One*, translated by Catherine Porter with Carolyn Burke (Cornell University Press, 1985), pp. 170–97.

50 Christine Holmlund, 'The Lesbian, the Mother and the Heterosexual lover: Irigaray's Recodings of Difference', *Feminist Studies,* 17(2) (1991), p. 288.

51 See Whitford, *Luce Irigaray,* ed. cit., pp. 75–97.

52 Irigaray, *L'Ethique de la Différence Sexuelle* (Minuit, 1984), p. 66. Cited by Holmlund, op. cit., p. 239.

53 Wittig, 'The Straight Mind' and 'One is Not Born a Woman', in *The Straight Mind,* ed. cit., pp. 32, 20.

54 See Butler, *Gender Trouble,* ed. cit., pp. 111–23; and Fuss, *Essentially Speaking,* ed. cit., pp. 41–53.

55 See Faderman, *Odd Girls and Twilight Lovers*, ed. cit., pp. 246–307; and Cherry Smyth, *Lesbians Talk Queer Notions* (Scarlet Press, 1992).

56 See Sedgwick, op. cit., pp. 37–41.

57 See Chapter 1, note 17.

58 See Sedgwick's discussion of the concept of 'homosexual panic' successfully employed in American law courts to defend queer-bashers (op. cit., pp. 18–22); and the feature on the new Colorado anti-gay law in *The Guardian*, 16 January 1993, p. 15.

59 DeLynn, 1991, pp. 236–7.

60 Faderman, *Odd Girls and Twilight Lovers*, ed. cit., pp. 274–84.

61 Mitchell, *Psychoanalysis and Feminism* (Pantheon, 1974).

62 Rose, *Sexuality in the Field of Vision* (Verso, 1986).

63 Benjamin, *The Bonds of Love: Psychoanalysis, Feminism, and the Problem of Domination* (Pantheon, 1988).

64 Quoted in Susan Ardill and Sue O'Sullivan, 'Upsetting an apple-cart: Difference, Desire and Lesbian Sadomasochism', *Feminist Review*, 23 (1986), p. 51.

65 Benjamin, 'Master and Slave: The Fantasy of Erotic Domination', ed. cit., p. 308.

66 Nestle, *A Restricted Country* (Firebrand, 1987), p. 148.

67 For reference to these conferences see Ardill and O'Sullivan, 'Upsetting an Applecart', ed. cit., p. 42–3; and Elizabeth Wilson, 'The Context of "Between Pleasure and Danger": The Barnard Conference on Sexuality', *Feminist Review,* 13 (1983), pp. 35–41.

68 Ardill and O'Sullivan, 'Upsetting an Applecart', ed. cit., p. 40.

69 Benjamin, 'Master and Slave', ed. cit., p. 308.

70 This is illustrated by Gayle Rubin, 'Thinking Sex: Notes for a Radical Theory of the Politics of Sexuality' in Carole S. Vance (ed.) *Pleasure and Danger: Exploring Female Sexuality* (Routledge and Kegan Paul, 1984), pp. 267–319.

71 See Faderman, *Odd Girls and Twilight Lovers*, ed. cit., pp. 246–70.

72 Susan Ardill and Sue O'Sullivan, 'Upsetting an Applecart', ed. cit., p. 40.

73 Elizabeth Wilson, 'The Context of "Between Pleasure and Danger"', ed. cit., p. 38.

74 Modleski, *Feminism Without Women*, ed. cit., p. 152.

75 SAMOIS (ed.) *Coming to Power: Writings and Graphics on Lesbian S/M* (Alyson, 1982), p. 185.

76 See Ardill and O'Sullivan, 'Upsetting an Applecart', ed. cit., pp. 52–3. See also Mike MacNair, 'The Contradictory Politics of SM', in *Coming on Strong*, ed. cit., pp. 147–62.

77 Kawash, 'Macho Sluts: It's a White Thing?', paper given at the Gay and Lesbian Studies Conference, Rutgers University, 1 November 1991. p. 6.

78 Modleski, *Feminism Without Women*, ed. cit., p. 155.

79 Nestle, *A Restricted Country*, ed. cit., p. 101.

80 For reference to butch–femme identification see Jeffreys, 'Butch and Femme', ed. cit., pp. 162–81; and Madeline Davis and Elizabeth Lapovsky Kennedy, 'Oral History and the Study of Sexuality in the Lesbian Community, Buffalo, New York, 1940–60', in Martin Bauml Duberman, Martha Vicinus and George Chauncey, jr. (eds) *Hidden from History: Reclaiming the Gay and Lesbian Past* (Penguin, 1991), pp. 426–40.

81 Wilson, 'Gayness and Liberalism', in Sandra Allen, Lee Sanders and Jan Wallis (eds) *Conditions of Illusion: Papers from the Women's Movement* (Feminist Books, 1974), pp. 113–14.

82 For reference to these different interpretations see Susan Ardill and Sue O'Sullivan, 'Butch/Femme Obsessions', *Feminist Review*, 34 (1990), pp. 79–85; and Sue-Ellen Case, 'Towards a Butch-Femme Aesthetic', in Lynda Hart (ed.) *Making a Spectacle: Feminist Essays on Contemporary Women's Theatre* (University of Michigan Press, 1989), pp. 282–97.

83 See Off Pink Publishing, *Bisexual Lives* (1988), pp. 13–14, 49; and Mariana Valverde, *Sex, Power and Pleasure* (Toronto, Canada, Women's Press, 1985), p. 117.

84 Stacey Young discusses these stereotypes and prejudices in 'Breaking Silence about the "B-Word": Bisexual Identity and Lesbian-Feminist Discourse', in *Closer to Home*, ed. cit., pp. 75–87.

85 For information about British groups and help-lines see the features by Sue George and Maev Kennedy in *The Guardian*, 17 September 1991, p. 37, and 4 September 1992, p. 27. Lesbian lines will also provide information. For reference to the phone numbers of British lesbian lines, see note 4.

86 Weise, *Closer to Home*, ed. cit., pp. 3–16.

87 See Smyth, op. cit., pp. 1–49; and Bobby Pickering, 'Queer Street Fighters', *The Guardian*, 8 September 1992, p. 17.

88 See the letters from Chris White and Frances Gillard in *The Guardian*, 17 September 1992, p. 21.

89 Comment by Maria Maggenti, quoted by Smyth, op. cit., p. 35.

90 See Faderman, *Odd Girls and Twilight Lovers*, ed. cit., pp. 240–2.

91 See Inge Blackman and Kathryn Perry, 'Skirting the Issue: Lesbian Fashion for the 1990s', *Feminist Review,* 34 (1990), pp. 67–78; and Elizabeth Wilson, 'Deviant Dress', *Feminist Review*, 35 (1990), pp. 67–74.

92 Zimmerman, 'Lesbians Like This and That', ed. cit., p. 3.

93 Fuss, *Essentially Speaking*, ed. cit., pp. 42–5.

94 Butler, 'Imitation and Gender Insubordination', in Fuss (ed.) *Inside Out: Lesbian Theories, Gay Theories* (Routledge, 1991), pp. 13–31.

95 Case, 'Toward a Butch–Femme Aesthetic', ed. cit., pp. 283–99.
96 Snitow *et al.*, *Desire: The Politics of Sexuality*, ed. cit., p. 31.
97 Snitow and her co-authors comment on the way 'the conflicting notions of sex as liberating or oppressive' recur in nineteenth- and twentieth-century discussions of sex (op. cit., p. 17).

3

Political fictions

The women sit in circles talking. They are passing telegrams along
battle-lines, telling each other stories that will not put them to sleep,
recognising allies under the disguise of femininity.

(Michèle Roberts 1978: 186)

The lesbian writer and her texts

A key episode in May Sarton's *A Reckoning* (1978), an example of the
lesbian political fiction discussed in this chapter, centres on a conversation
between Harriet Moors, a young writer who has just completed a lesbian
novel, and Laura Spelman, the editor of the firm which she hopes will
publish it. The two women's approaches to the novel differ markedly.
While Laura is chiefly interested in its literary aspects, such as the verisimili-
tude of the characters, Harriet is preoccupied with matters of a personal
kind. She tells Laura that, in order to avoid upsetting her parents who are
unaware of her lesbian orientation, she will have to publish under a
pseudonym. When Laura urges her to have the courage of her convictions
and use her own name, arguing that the use of the signature will increase
the impact of the book, she points out that she is taking an immense risk in
publishing it at all. To do so will probably have dire consequences for her
partner, who is a school teacher, since it may result in her losing her job.
Torn between a desire to see the work which she has created in print and a
sense of loyalty to her partner, Harriet despondently observes, 'If I publish
the book it's the end of us.'[1]

The conversation between the two women and the kind of issues which
it raises are relevant to the lesbian political fiction of the 1970s and early
1980s in general. In the first place, the episode introduces us to the figure
of the lesbian writer and some of the problems which confront her.
The image of her as a figure with strong feminist allegiances who regards

lesbianism in terms of sexual politics and seeks to promote the interests of lesbians as a group originated in this particular period. Zimmerman, summing up its salient features, points out that:

> Lesbian writers, unlike those writers who incorporate a lesbian character or lesbian scene in a novel, are women who identify themselves in some way with the lesbian community. They may identify themselves as lesbians in their creative writing (by stressing autobiographical elements, for example) or in biographies or interviews. They may do so through their choice of publisher, since certain presses are exclusively or primarily lesbian or gay.[2]

The episode from *A Reckoning* mentioned above highlights, in fact, the problematic aspect of the lesbian writer's role and the conflicts between personal and political interests which she often confronts. Subsequent episodes investigate another related theme: the effect which lesbian writing has on the female reader. They show how the experience of reading Harriet's novel, in conjunction with certain other events, prompts Laura to face up to and re-evaluate the woman-identified relationships which are a feature of her own past.

As well as focusing attention on the figure of the lesbian writer and her relationship with a prospective editor, the episode also pinpoints certain attributes of the texts which she produces. As is evident from the connection which Harriet makes between publishing and Coming Out, lesbian novels are frequently autobiographical in impulse. They involve a particularly complex interplay between life and art, and thus raise crucial questions relating to the signature. Even if they are not, in actual fact, autobiographical, they are generally thought to be, for, in the homophobic culture in which we live, 'It is invariably assumed that anyone who writes on lesbian subjects is herself lesbian.'[3] Readers of lesbian fiction tend to identify the author with the characters whom she creates and to envisage a unified authorial voice dominating and controlling the text. These assumptions, though questioned and problematized by postmodernist critics, are of vital importance to readers who identify as lesbians, since they offer them a means of personal affirmation and social integration. This explains, as Reina Lewis argues, why lesbian writers and critics:

> tend to return to the liberal humanist idea of the subject. It is all very well being told that the sovereign controlling subject is dead, but for groups who were denied access to the authoritative reading and writing position the first time round, there is a very real need to occupy it now. As lesbians we want role models, we want to feel part of a cultural tradition, to know that we have a history of creativity, one that speaks to our experience and concerns.[4]

The refusal of many writers of lesbian political fiction to comply with postmodernist concepts of 'the decentered text' and 'the death of the author', combined with the relegation of the texts which they produce to the category of 'minority literature', help to account for the neglect they suffer and the adverse criticism they often receive. Fiction of this kind, though popular with non-academic readers who eagerly scan the lists of the American Naiad and the British Onlywomen Presses in search of new titles, is generally denigrated or ignored by academics. Other factors too contribute to its neglect. Critical studies of contemporary women's criticism and fiction frequently reflect and reproduce the heterosexist perspectives of the dominant culture. As a consequence, they tend to ignore the specificity of lesbian writing and, by subsuming it under the heading of 'feminist' or 'confessional' texts, marginalize or render invisible its lesbian content. Critics guilty of this practice include Cora Kaplan who, in an essay on feminist criticism, encompasses the lesbian writing of the 1970s in the generalizing phrase 'those texts [which] were part of the ongoing debate of the social movement of which we were a part';[5] and Judi M. Roller who, in discussing Piercy's *Small Changes* in her study of the feminist novel, fails to mention that the work, which is organized around the contrasting experiences and values of the heterosexual Miriam and the lesbian Beth, has a significant lesbian component.[6] This particular omission is symptomatic of Roller's general failure to acknowledge the contribution which lesbian perspectives and ideas have made to contemporary women's fiction.

The lesbian fiction of the 1970s and early 1980s has aroused, more surprisingly, little interest from critics who work in the field of Lesbian and Gay Studies.[7] Critics working in these areas, influenced by postmodern trends in criticism, frequently prefer to construct lesbian or what they term 'perverse' readings of texts from the dominant culture rather than to focus on texts which treat lesbian characters and themes. Mandy Merck, whose study *Perversions* (1993) exemplifies this perspective, implies that the former critical approach is more radical than the latter – and goes so far as to question the value of novels and films which treat lesbian characters and cater for a lesbian readership. She condemns the positive images of lesbianism which they often create, dismissing them as mere 'narcissistic projections'.[8] Here, I disagree with Merck. In my opinion, room exists for a variety of different styles of lesbian writing and criticism. The positive images created by writers such as Marge Piercy, Elizabeth Riley and Nancy Toder served to inspire and empower readers – especially in the early stages of the Lesbian Feminist Movement when lesbian culture and community were in an embryonic state and at their most fragile. They provided an effective strategy to challenge and counter the negative and bigoted stereotypes of lesbianism inherited from the first half of the century. And while lesbian and 'perverse' readings of texts certainly serve a useful function, so too do discussions of novels and films which are explicitly lesbian. To praise one at the expense of the other and to imply that critics should concern themselves only with lesbian readings can result in the neglect of lesbian culture. It gives the impression that lesbian novels and films are too trivial to merit critical comment, in this way promoting the marginalization which they already suffer. It also reproduces the elitist attitudes and the emphasis on hierarchy in literary and critical discourse associated with traditional concepts of the canon.

The few critics who do focus on fictional texts which are explicitly lesbian frequently disparage them, unfairly in my view, for lacking emotional tension[9] or being stylistically unadventurous.[10] The novels discussed in this chapter illustrate the injustice of these charges. As well as being emotionally complex, they exemplify a variety of different modes of writing. These include the experimental use of multiple narrators and dialect in Caeia March's *Three Ply Yarn* (1986), the utopian fantasy of Gearhart's *The Wanderground* (1979), and the so-called realism of Elizabeth Riley's *All That False Instruction* (1975) and Anna Wilson's *Altogether Elsewhere* (1985). I say 'so-called' because, as I and other critics argue,[11] the selective treatment of character and events and the emphasis placed on subjective experience, which characterize works of feminist realism, have little in common with the representation of a transparent reflection of reality associated with the classic nineteenth-century realist novel. Its practitioners are more interested in delineating subtleties of personal feeling and in treating themes relating to sexual politics than in giving a detailed description of a particular social scene or milieu.[12] As Zimmerman, commenting on the way lesbian fiction frequently subverts realist conventions, observes, 'Even the most conspicuously realistic texts of the 1980s lace their portrayal of reality with the myths of lesbian culture.[13] Moreover, the writer's choice of an ostensibly realist format is, in the majority of cases, by no means naive or unintelligent but is motivated by a belief in the social and political efficacy of literature. It enables her to establish direct and intimate contact with the reader, and signals that she is interested in exploring and conveying issues and ideas of a social and political kind.

A distinctive feature of the lesbian fiction of the 1970s and early 1980s is the readiness of writers to appropriate concepts from lesbian feminist theory and rework them in fictional form. Many of these concepts will be familiar to the reader from the discussion of lesbian theory in the previous chapter. Lesbian theory is, as we have seen, a field which is immensely rich and varied. As a result, writers find it a vital source of inspiration and intellectual stimulus. Some of the ideas incorporated in the texts discussed, such as the political significance of Coming Out and the belief that the lesbian feminist identity represents a challenge to patriarchal power and male-defined images of femininity, relate to the individual female subject and her development. Others, in contrast, focus on social relations between women and are relevant to women as a group. Among the latter are Rich's theory of lesbian continuum, and the idea, generally accepted by lesbian feminists, that lesbian community forms the hub and mainstay of the Women's Movement. Writers working in the 1970s and 1980s employ, as we shall see, a variety of different narrative strategies and structures to explore and convey these ideas.

The novel of self-discovery

One of the most popular kinds of lesbian fiction produced in the 1970s and early 1980s is the novel of self-discovery or, as it is sometimes termed, the 'Coming Out novel'.[14] It has achieved international status among English-speaking writers as a vehicle for lesbian themes and ideas and is represented by works of fiction as diverse as *A Piece of the Night* (1978) by the British Michèle Roberts, *On Strike Against God* (1980) by the American Joanna Russ and *All That False Instruction* (1975) by the Australian Elizabeth Riley. Critical analyses of the novel of self-discovery generally centre on the protagonist's subjectivity and underestimate, in my opinion, its significant social dimension.[15] The importance of this is illustrated by the three novels cited above. While differing markedly in style, and in the portrayal of the protagonist and her circumstances, they have in common the fact that they describe her progress of psychological development as by no means solitary. Her discovery of her lesbian orientation, which is the focal point of the novels, whether represented in essentialist terms as something which she uncovers from the recesses of her psyche or depicted from a constructionist point of view as something which she, consciously or unconsciously, creates, relates very clearly to her interaction with the world at large. It depends, on the one hand, on her acts of resistance to the dominant culture and, on the other, on the supportive relationship which she establishes with the lesbian feminist community.[16] The latter may be represented by a group of women or, alternatively, by a single friend or partner. Whichever the case, it plays a crucial role in her psychological growth and powers of self-definition.

In discussing the lesbian novel of self-discovery, critics have pinpointed a number of different metaphors and motifs, such as re-birth, awakening and the journey[17] as central to its design. One which they neglect to mention is the motif of 'unlearning' which informs Riley's *All That False Instruction*. The concept of unlearning, unpromising though it at first appears as the basis for a fictional text, plays an important part in the experience of many women who identify as lesbian. In order to emphasize the strength of heterosexual conventions and the difficulty which women experience in liberating themselves from them, Riley bases her novel on the assumption that the first step towards achieving a lesbian identity and way of life is to problematize and reject the oppressive stereotypes of femininity promoted by the dominant culture. By so doing, she inverts the premise of the conventional *bildungsroman*, which portrays the male heterosexual hero learning a series of positive lessons in life, and emphasizes the more complex and tortuous process which lesbian education involves. *All That False Instruction* reveals a number of points of interest, literary as well as political. As well as illustrating the way writers anticipate or rework concepts from lesbian feminist theory, popularizing them in fictional form, it offers an insight into the strategies which practitioners of feminist realism employ to establish contact with the reader and involve her imaginatively in the production of the narrative.

To readers looking for a story of lesbian romance *All That False Instruction* may prove something of a disappointment, since, as is the case with other novels written in the early years of the Lesbian Feminist Movement,[18] the text operates more as an indictment of the sexism and homophobia prevalent in contemporary society than as a sentimental tale of lesbian love. Having witnessed friends and acquaintances suffer ridicule and persecution and survived such experiences themselves, writers understandably felt the need, one which was partly therapeutic in impulse and partly sociopolitical, to record them in print. By treating them in fictional form, they achieve the twin goals of alerting the reader to their existence and exorcising, to a degree, their oppressive effect. Although the emphasis which Riley places on lesbian suffering and victimization appears to conform on a cursory reading to 'the anguish that not only dares to speak its name but dares to bare its wounds'[19] criticized by Elizabeth Wilson, in actual fact the novel offers the reader an experience which is notably more complex. The focus on lesbian suffering in *All That False Instruction*, as is the case with other novels published in the 1970s,[20] is not merely personal in nature but serves, on the contrary, as the base for an exposé and critique of the bigotry and injustices which lesbians encounter as a group.

The novel's storyline is relatively simple. Employing a first person narrative, Riley recounts the adventures of Maureen Craig who, having succeeded in escaping from her emotionally-stifling home in the Australian outback where she lived with her dominating mother and weak-willed brother Ken, embarks on a course of study at the local university. The relationship which she forms with Libby, a fellow student, results in her discovering her lesbian orientation. The involvement, however, instead of bringing the two girls happiness, terminates disastrously in scenes of betrayal and recrimination. Libby, influenced by the homophobic attitudes of her peers, deserts Maureen, leaving her to face the ridicule of her classmates who deride her as a cripple and a freak. The relationships with women which Maureen forms subsequently, though fulfilling in the early stages, are represented as similarly emotionally fraught and short-lived. We watch them being distorted and destroyed by the lack of a supportive social network and the need for secrecy and subterfuge, which the lesbian stigma imposes.

This depressing account of the isolation experienced by the young lesbian in the Australia of the 1960s acts as a foil to the optimistic note on which the novel concludes. The events which occur in the final pages signal to the reader that in other areas of the world, if not yet in Australia, the Lesbian Feminist Movement is starting to emerge. While attending a local party, Maureen happens to encounter Jody, a visitor from New York. Jody is a representative of the burgeoning Lesbian Feminist Movement and, in contrast to the other women whom Maureen knows, regards lesbianism as the signifier of feminism and associates it with liberation. Inspired by her example, Maureen decides to cut her losses and leave her native land. The novel concludes with her setting sail for foreign climes, in search of lesbian community and a more fulfilling way of life.

The idea that lesbian identity and existence depend on the female subject unlearning and rejecting the misogynistic definitions of femininity and lesbianism promoted by contemporary society which Maureen's trajectory reflects, is, as we have seen, a central tenet of Radicalesbians' 'The Woman Identified Woman'. The novel's representation of lesbian experience displays, in fact, interesting analogies with the essay. Like the lesbian portrayed by Radicalesbians, Maureen emerges from the text as the archetypal feminist revolutionary. Living as she does in the pre-feminist era of the 1960s, she does not, of course, identify as lesbian feminist. However, to quote Radicalesbians, her 'needs and actions, over a period of years bring her into painful conflict with people, situations, the accepted ways of thinking, feeling and behaving, until she is in a state of continual war with everything around her'.[21] In her dissatisfaction with and ultimate rejection of male-defined constructs of femininity, she resembles the lesbian in 'The Woman Identified Woman' who, though 'she may not be fully conscious of the political implications of what for her began as personal necessity, on some level has not been able to accept the limitations and oppression laid on her by the most basic role of her society – the female role' (p. 240).

In employing Maureen as the mouthpiece for a critique of male-defined codes of femininity, Riley also expresses in fictional form the concept of the lesbian's role as critic of patriarchal attitudes and values articulated by Bunch and other lesbian feminists. They regard the lesbian's woman-identified perspective and marginalized social position as giving her 'a specific vantage-point from which to criticize and analyse the politics, language and culture of patriarchy'.[22] Maureen's protests and acts of rebellion against sexual inequalities and male expectations of femininity commence at an early age. As a child, she resents belonging to what she rightly perceives to be 'the drudging half of the world'[23] and stubbornly resists her mother's efforts to make her do the housework while her brother is excused such chores. She also challenges discrimination in education, insisting that, though she is female, she merits a place at university. And when, in the second half of the novel, she is reluctantly persuaded to engage in sexual relations with men, Riley utilizes her frustrating encounters to expose the prevalence of the double standard. Criticism focuses on the way the male partner expects the female to remain passive while he initiates and directs the love-making. In an episode which treats ideas similar to those articulated by Koedt,[24] Maureen criticizes the male propensity to regard penetrative sex as the only acceptable form of sexual practice and to condemn clitoral sex as perverse and unnatural. Here, as in works of lesbian theory,[25] the lesbian is portrayed as seeing through and rejecting male-defined concepts of 'the natural' and 'the normal', and exposing them as oppressive constructs.

As well as challenging male-defined concepts of femininity and sexual practice, the novel also utilizes the incidents of persecution which Maureen suffers to expose bigoted stereotypes of lesbianism. The dismissal of lesbian relationships as a 'dead-end business' (Riley 1981: 83), voiced by one of Maureen's classmates, and the representation of the lesbian as an outcast, witch (p. 101), monster (p. 241) and carrier of infectious disease (p. 101), are some of the lesbophobic images explored. Riley acknowledges their oppressive effect and shows that they originate in ignorance and fear. The stereotyping of the lesbian as 'mannish' (p. 173), and the derogatory misrepresentation of lesbian love as 'lust', (p. 135) are also challenged.

Another topic which links *All That False Instruction* to the theoretical writing of the 1970s is *lesbian feminist community*. The novel highlights its social and psychological importance by focusing, paradoxically, on its absence. For much of her youth Maureen knows no other women who identify as lesbian. Libby and the various other women with whom she has brief affairs, though willing to have sex with her, give her little companionship or support. They quickly succumb to the pressures of the lesbian stigma and desert her for male lovers. However, despite lack of visible evidence, Maureen is convinced that other women who identify as lesbian do exist. She also perceives that the frequent break-downs of her relationships and the conflicts which beset them stem not from her personal inadequacies but from the lack of a supportive social context. Thus when Jody, the representative of lesbian feminist community, eventually makes an appearance in the narrative, the references which she makes to the topic do not fall on deaf ears. Maureen, and through her mediation, the reader have already recognized its importance and given it some thought.

Another figure who plays a supportive role in Maureen's life is her heterosexual German friend, Inga Schmidt. As is apparent from her outspoken criticism of male sexism, Inga is portrayed as a potential feminist. She is unperturbed by Maureen's disclosure of her lesbian orientation, sympathizes with her isolated position and, ignoring the lesbian stigma, acts as her confidante and ally.

However, Maureen's most reliable and consistent confidante is neither Inga nor any of the other characters but the reader – or rather the community of feminist readers to whom the novel is addressed. By employing a confessional, first-person narrative, Riley encodes a feminist readership into the text. The contact which Maureen establishes with it compensates to a degree for the lack of feminist community in her life and the failure of her personal relationships.

While introducing ideas which are basic to lesbian theory and conveying them to the reader in an accessible, popular format, *All That False Instruction* also reproduces, unavoidably perhaps, the contradictions and limitations of this theory. Like other works of lesbian fiction published in the 1970s and early 1980s, it reveals little understanding of female heterosexuality but crassly dismisses it as a form of false consciousness. Sexual relationships with men are represented throughout as something which women 'endure' (p. 214), rather than enjoy.

Bisexuality is another topic which the novel misrepresents, by treating it simplistically and unfairly. As in other works of fiction with a similar lesbian feminist viewpoint, such as Toder's *Choices* and Barbara Wilson's *Ambitious Women* (1982), the female bisexual is contemptuously portrayed as a 'failed' lesbian and a traitor to the lesbian cause.[26] Libby and the other women with whom Maureen has brief affairs, are represented as weak-willed characters who succumb easily to the pressures of convention and vacillate uncertainly between male and female lovers. In political fiction of this kind, as in the lesbian feminist theory the perspectives of which it shares, lesbianism tends to function as the signifier of feminism. This precludes or, at any rate, works against, the sympathetic delineation of other sexual identifications and desires.

Lesbian continuum

A feature of lesbian theory which had a major influence on the lesbian fiction of the 1908s is the concept of lesbian continuum, formulated by Rich.[27] Lesbian continuum and the cluster of ideas which it involves contribute, as we saw in the previous chapter, to the belief in a uniquely female sphere and vision articulated by the Cultural Feminist Movement. They challenge the narrow sexual definition of the sign *lesbian* coined by the male sexologists by expanding its meaning to include forms of woman-identified experience, such as female friendship and feminist camaraderie, which are not overtly sexual. Lesbian continuum has important political implications. It represents lesbian existence as a form of resistance to patriarchal power. In addition, by placing all women who have experienced incidents of woman–identification on the lesbian continuum irrespective of their professed sexual orientation, it attempts to heal the rift between lesbian feminists and their heterosexual sisters, which developed as a result of the position of extreme separatism advocated by the Political Lesbian Movement. The concept, though praised by some critics as politically empowering, has also met with criticism. Its critics accuse it of reductively conflating the terms 'lesbian', 'feminist' and 'female'. They argue that it ignores the specificity of lesbian relationships by neglecting or undervaluing its sexual dimension.[28]

Whatever its shortcomings from a theoretical point of view, lesbian continuum and the debates which it has provoked have had an invigorating effect on the writing of fiction. By focusing attention on themes of female friendship and social relations between women, they have encouraged writers to move away from the narrow focus on a single female figure who, by acknowledging her lesbian orientation and forming relationships with other women, resists male-defined expectations of femininity and challenges homophobic prejudice. They prompt them to focus instead on a group of women, exploring the links between them and examining their points of affinity and difference. The interest in feminist and lesbian feminist community, reflected in the novel of self-discovery in the emphasis placed on the protagonist's involvements with other female characters and the relationship which she establishes with the reader, becomes, in texts treating lesbian continuum, increasingly explicit and central.

According to Rich, lesbian continuum involves 'a range – through each woman's life and throughout history – of woman-identified experience'.[29] Some fictional texts, in consonance with this description, explore both the personal and the historical facets of the continuum. As well as depicting female friendships and relationships, they compare and contrast constructs of lesbianism from different periods and seek to re-create and celebrate a lost tradition of women's creativity and culture. The three works of fiction discussed in this section illustrate the varied treatment accorded themes of this kind by writers from different social and ethnic backgrounds.

Ann Oosthuizen's *Loneliness and Other Lovers* (1981), though written too early to be influenced by Rich's ideas, introduces cultural feminist concepts of woman-identification and female culture which reveal connections with them. The novel's interest lies in the detailed, carefully documented account it gives of the reasons which prompt women to cease making men the focus of their lives and, instead, transfer their love and allegiance to women.

The novel opens with Jean, a woman in her mid-40s, leaving her middle-class home in the provinces and, acting on information supplied by her teenage son, moving into a squat in the London borough of Camden. Here she meets Sara who, unlike herself, is unmarried and is accustomed to an independent, urban lifestyle. Although at the start of the novel the two identify as heterosexual, their growing affection for one another, combined with the interests they share, bring them increasingly close. Both have experience of male-exploitation. They encounter sexist behaviour, the novel illustrates, not only from men with traditional 'family' values but also from the pseudo-liberated men whom they meet at the squat. Their friendship deepens, strengthened by acts of mutual support and by participation in feminist cultural and social activities. They visit women's bookshops together, attend a feminist conference, and become involved in running a group for young women. In an episode which articulates the novel's woman-identified perspective, Sara acknowledges the contradiction which she feels in continuing to relate to men while devoting her political, practical and emotional energies to women. She tells Jean that, while the outer circle of her life is filled with activities 'mostly with women, the trouble is that the small space is often filled by a man – and somehow the two can't coexist. You have to choose, one or the other.'[30] The final pages signal that the two choose to remain together – and give their allegiance to women.

Oosthuizen's decision to conclude the novel with Sara and Jean apparently on the verge of becoming lovers is open to different readings. It may be criticized on the grounds that it enables her to avoid confronting and representing the sexual aspect of lesbianism. Alternatively, it may be accepted as suiting the concept of woman-identification which is central to the text. By avoiding depicting Jean's and Sara's involvement in terms which are narrowly sexual, Oosthuizen, like Rich, expands the meaning of the sign *lesbian* and encourages female readers who have experience of woman-identified relationships but do not regard themselves as lesbian to empathize and identify with it.

A novel published some years later which is structured on the concept of lesbian continuum is March's *Three Ply Yarn* (1986). In the account which she gives of writing it, March describes herself as seeking to treat both the personal and historical aspects of lesbian culture as they relate to British working-class life.[31] The text is organized around two groups of women, the one rural in context and the other urban. It explores the connections which they form with one another and with family and friends. The introduction of three different narrators gives the text a decentered appearance and suits its focus on female interaction and women's community.

Dee and Dora, evacuees from wartime London, spend their childhood in the countryside. They form a relationship and, on hearing that their parents have been killed in a bombing raid, run away together, surviving financially by finding employment in the local hotels. In contrast, the two sisters Essie and Lottie grow up in the Northern town of Densley and have a close-knit family life. Grandma Clegg, whose skill at grafting knitting wool provides the inspiration for the novel's title and the interweaving narratives which comprise the text, is portrayed as the background of the family. The anecdotes and stories which she tells remain with Essie long after she has left home and is working as a school-teacher. They motivate her to write and, in an attempt to discover her roots and remedy the loneliness caused by the process of upward mobility on which she has embarked, record her family history. Her jottings and diary entries are a vehicle for the historical facet of lesbian continuum. They introduce us to, among other characters, the dynamic figure of Red Heather, a 1930s political activist, and her various involvements with women.

In treating the historical dimension of lesbian continuum, March succeeds in achieving a balance between an essentialist approach, which focuses on the continuity of lesbian experience, and a constructionist one which recognizes change in lesbian roles and lifestyle.[32] Emphasis is placed on the way constructs of lesbianism differ from period to period and on the different routes which women take in adopting a lesbian identification. Dee and Dora live an isolated existence for many years. Cuddling in bed, enjoying 'the comfort and the kisses',[33] they regard their relationship in a purely personal light and even lack a language to define it. Their circle widens when they encounter the group of women centering on the local inn. Here they discover the complexities of the lesbian social scene and meet women who identify as butch or femme. The advent of the Lesbian Feminist Movement in the 1970s brings about further transformations. The political perspective which it introduces is described as beneficial in the respect that it makes lesbians socially visible and encourages them to unite to challenge prejudice and discrimination. However, it also gives rise to friction and discord. Misunderstandings and conflicts occur between the new 'political' lesbian feminists, and the women who identified as lesbian prior to the Movement.

Another topic which achieved prominence in the 1980s and receives attention in *Three Ply Yarn* is race.[34] In contrast to works of fiction produced in the 1970s, the majority of which focused exclusively on white characters and their activities, the novel seeks to explore the interaction between racial oppression and forms of discrimination relating to gender and sexual orientation. The episodes portraying the white Dee raising her lover's black daughter Izzie in a British provincial town in the 1960s focus on inter-racial involvements and illustrate the stigma frequently attached to them. The hardships and incidents of prejudice which the two women encounter are powerfully described. Dee experiences loneliness and misunderstanding on account of the invisibility of her lesbianism, whereas Izzie is ridiculed by her classmates because her blackness is only too visible.

Three Ply Yarn challenges the view expressed by some critics that writers of lesbian fiction, particularly those working in the 1970s and early 1980s, are uninterested in experimenting with form and create texts which are lacking in art.[35] Its utilization of multiple narrators and modes of writing traditionally defined as feminine, such as diary entries and letters which, since they are personal and nonliterary, are often dismissed by the mainstream critical discourse as trivial, gives the text a fractured, episodic appearance. These modes of writing, as well as reflecting the 'dailiness'[36] of women's lives and the intimacy and fragility of their relationships, serve to create links between women of different generations. Essie's diary entries introduce us to the determined, strong-willed women who peopled her childhood. Letter-writing, as well as functioning in the novel as a means of communication between friends and lovers, provides a record of the romantic attachments and lesbian relationships which flourished in earlier periods. The novel concludes aptly with the discovery of the cache of letters which Essie's mother wrote to Red Heather, who, we discover, was her lover.

As in other novels centering on woman–identification and female cultural activities, such as Oosthuizen's *Loneliness and Other Lovers* and Sarton's *A Reckoning*, emphasis is placed on the secretive, concealed nature of both women's relationships and female culture itself. Dee's earliest memories centre on a 'secret place . . . in Dorset, near the wild violets' (March 1986: 7,1), which she frequented with Dora. She comments, 'We were a secret people. Our loving had to be secret' (p. 7). Essie likewise sees her writing as a surreptitious activity, describing the den where she works as 'my secret room, a place to hide away' (March 1986: 15). Influenced by lesbian feminist ideals of candour and political directness, the trajectory of the female characters reflects a movement away from secrecy in personal relationships and cultural practice to a focus on self-revelation and disclosure. Essie's personal development illustrates this. She uncovers and discusses forgotten aspects of women's lives at the local history group which she attends and, on discovering her lesbian orientation, Comes Out to her friends and family.

Three Ply Yarn, though originally conceived and skilfully crafted, reveals a number of flaws and inconsistencies. Like other works of lesbian fiction produced in the 1970s and early 1980s, the text is impaired by an excessive concern with political correctness. Women are portrayed throughout as morally superior to men, and lesbian relationships are represented as generally caring and unaggressive. Male sexuality, in contrast, is associated with violence and a dependence on pornographic stimulation. No mention is made of the fact that some lesbians enjoy porn – or would do if materials with a lesbian slant were more easily available![37]

Another problem with the novel is that, with the aim of achieving a neat denouement and concluding on a positive note, March portrays a disproportionate number of female characters whom she initially depicts as heterosexual as unexpectedly 'seeing the light' and undergoing a lesbian 'conversion'. Their former heterosexual attachments are devalued by being unconvincingly dismissed as motivated by the need for economic survival. This appears to reflect the essentialist notion that the majority of women are really lesbian at heart – and that, when the layers of heterosexual conditioning are stripped away, a lesbian sexuality will be revealed.

In contrast to *Three Ply Yarn*, which treats both the historical and the personal aspects of lesbian continuum, 'The Threshing Floor' (1986), a novella by the London-based black writer Barbara Burford, concentrates

solely on the latter. Rich's description of lesbian continuum as encompassing a spectrum of woman-identified involvements, ranging from 'the infant
suckling at her mother's breast, to the grown woman experiencing orgas-
mic sensations while suckling her own child . . . to the woman dying at
ninety, touched and handled by woman' (p. 54), makes an appropriate
introduction to it, by bringing together the contraries of mothering and
death which Burford explores.

'The Threshing Floor' opens with Hannah, a black woman who works
as a glass blower in rural Kent, mourning the death of her white lover Jenny
who has recently died of cancer. As well as exploring the racist treatment
which she experiences from both the local community and Jenny's dominating mother, it traces the progress which she makes from a state of
introverted grief to a re-involvement in work and the forming of a new
relationship. Jenny's death functions, in fact, as a catalyst. It prompts
Hannah to confront and re-evaluate certain formative experiences in her
past, along with her present relationships with friends and co-workers. One
of the topics which she feels forced to confront is the connection between
lesbianism and mother-daughter relations, a theme discussed by lesbian
feminist theorists.[38] Having been abandoned by her mother at an early age
and brought up in an institution, she admits that she sought in the relationship with Jenny maternal tenderness as well as sexual passion. However
Jenny, who has had to cope with her own mother's emotional demands,
rejects her attitude of dependence. 'I will *not* be a mother to you', she tells
her firmly – and encourages her to cultivate the art of self-nurture.[39] The
motif of mothering, which is central to the text, takes a new slant when
Marah, a black fellow artist whom Hannah meets after Jenny's death and to
whom she is sexually attracted, mentions to her that her plans for the future
include having a baby. She will either adopt one, she says, or use the
services of a donor (p. 210). This reference to lesbian motherhood, coin-
ciding as it does with Hannah's recovery from mourning Jenny's death and
with her process of emotional 'rebirth', completes the sequence of ideas
relating to birth and mothering, psychological as well as physical, around
which the narrative revolves.

As is the case with the two other fictional texts discussed in this section,
female cultural and artistic activities are topics of central interest in 'The
Threshing Floor'. Emphasis is placed, moreover, on their communal aspect.
Hannah's work as a glass-blower is represented as taking place in the context
of the Cantii Glass Cooperative, a separatist organization which she has
helped to found. Burford's approach to feminist community is by no means
idealized since, as well as illustrating its positive features, she also explores
incidents of friction and discord. Differences of race, financial privilege and
sexual orientation are depicted as giving rise, on occasion, to tensions and
conflicts. Feminist community, the novella indicates, is as fragile an achievement as the pieces of glass created by Hannah and her co-workers.

Lesbian community

Lesbian community, as is apparent from the references to it, both explicit and implicit, in the texts discussed above, is of major importance to the analysis of lesbianism produced by the Lesbian Feminist Movement. It ranks, with lesbian feminist identity and Coming Out, as a key concept in the 1970s theorization of lesbianism. In the writing of the period community is represented not only as a source of personal relationships and political support for the individual woman but also as the basis of a dynamic counter-culture which aims to challenge patriarchal values and institutions. Bunch, for example, in her influential essay 'Not For Lesbians Only' (1975) describes 'a critique of the institution and ideology of heterosexuality as a cornerstone of male supremacy', combined with 'a commitment to women as a political group',[40] as the twin pillars of lesbian feminist politics. Like Rich, she seeks to expand the significance of the sign *lesbian* by making it relevant to women in general. Treating lesbianism as the signifier of feminism, she and other theorists[41] argue that the critique of the dominant culture which the lesbian produces is relevant to all women, irrespective of their sexual orientation. They see the lesbian's woman-identified perspective and marginalized position as giving her a particularly acute insight into the injustices and abuses of patriarchy.

Analyses of this kind, combined with the lesbian feminist tendency to see all women as 'really lesbian' at heart which we have seen operating in March's *Three Ply Yarn*, help to explain why, in the theory and fiction of the 1970s and early 1980s, lesbian community and sisterhood have a habit of expanding and merging into the wider entities of feminist and even female community. This expansion, Elizabeth Wilson and Modleski argue,[42] has a confusing and reductive effect on theoretical discourse. Its effect on fiction, however, is distinctly liberating. It encourages the writer to portray a variety of female figures, including in her repertoire of characters not only women who identify as lesbian but also heterosexuals and bisexuals. It also prompts her to investigate the emotional and social interaction which occurs between women in a group context. Whereas in certain texts, such as Gearhart's *The Wanderground*, the author's desire to expand the significance of lesbian community and make it relevant to women as a group has the unfortunate consequence of reducing the female characters to a homogeneous bunch of woman-identified look-alikes, in more complex and intelligent ones, such as Piercy's *The High Cost of Living* (1978) and Anna Wilson's *Altogether Elsewhere* (1985), it gives rise to a welcome emphasis on female diversity.

Novels of this type, in keeping with the topos of lesbian community which they treat, frequently focus on feminist groups and organizations. Examples include Barbara Wilson's *Ambitious Women* (1982), and Lisa Alther's *Kinflicks* (1976) and *Other Women* (1984). As I have discussed these novels in detail elsewhere,[43] here I shall mention only their salient features.

Ambitious Women takes as its location a print-shop, run by the two central characters Allison and Holly, and a women's refuge where the former works on a voluntary basis. The novel highlights, in a somewhat schematized way, both the value and the fragility of women's community. To make the theme accessible to a wide female readership, Wilson concentrates on a group of women who differ in sexual orientation. She also highlights the fluidity of sexual identification and desire. Whereas Allison identifies as heterosexual throughout, Holly, her business partner, embarks on a relationship with another woman and changes her identification to lesbian. In the portrayal of the journalist Magda, the novel introduces the prejudiced representation of the female bisexual which is all too common in the fiction of the 1970s and early 1980s. Characterized as egocentric, unreliable and flirtatious, Magda epitomizes the disruptive and transgressive aspects of female sexuality.

Alther's *Kinflicks* and *Other Women* also introduces a variety of female characters and sexual identifications. The former is a novel of self-discovery which treats the popular sixties' theme of woman's quest for self-fulfilment through experimentation with life-style, sex and drugs. The heroine Ginny intersperses a series of involvements with men with a lesbian affair, which takes place in the context of a separatist hippie commune. The latter novel has a stronger lesbian focus, and reworks in fictional form the feminist debate about the advantages and disadvantages of therapy. The text concentrates on a number of encounters between Caroline, a lesbian mother, and her heterosexual analyst Hannah Burke. At the start, the two women adopt polarized positions and argue fiercely. Subsequently, however, as they start to appreciate one another's points of view, their attitudes become less intransigent.

Although the concept of lesbian community is as important today as it was in the early seventies, approaches towards it have not remained static but have altered considerably in the intervening years. Theorists writing at the start of the Lesbian Feminist Movement, when expectations of lesbian unity and success in challenging heterosexual conventions and institutions were at their most idealistic and naive, generally adopt a celebratory stance. Depicting lesbians as a homogeneous group, they represent the achievement of community as their chief goal. These ideas influence the structure and the development of their writing. A centrifugal movement from a focus on the individual to a focus on the group informs many of the essays, both feminist and lesbian feminist, produced in the period. Rich, for example, in 'Conditions for Work: The Common World of Woman' observes that, 'Feminism begins but cannot end with the discovery by the individual woman of her self-consciousness as a woman' and goes on to assert that 'our hope . . . depends on seeking and giving our allegiance to a community of women co-workers.'[44] Radicalesbians' 'The Woman Identified Woman' progresses, as we have seen, from the portrayal of the individual discovering her lesbian orientation in isolation, to an affirmation of the value of community and group participation: 'Only women can give to each other a new sense of self . . . *Together* we must find, reinforce and validate our authentic selves' (p. 245, italics added).

The view of lesbian community as representing a unified category, the members of which are all similarly committed to feminist aims and agree, moreover, on the strategies necessary to achieve them, was, of course, too unrealistic to remain unchallenged for long. The dogmatic insistence on political correctness and group-allegiance which it generated proved irksome to many women, while the principles of political commitment and self-sacrifice which it fostered, though inspiring in the abstract, were in many cases too extreme to be practical.[45] The difficulty of maintaining such high standards of behaviour either alienated women or, if they were sensitive souls, plunged them into an abyss of guilt and self-criticism. Sigrid Nielsen gives an illuminating insight into this process. In an autobiographical essay, aptly entitled 'Strange Days', she charts the downward curve from idealism to disillusion which she experienced while working in radical bookselling cooperatives in Edinburgh. She describes how a cluster of factors, including exhaustion from over-work, emotional isolation, political disagreements and a general breakdown in communication in the workplace, resulted in her suffering symptoms of fatigue and depression.[46] Her plight was exacerbated by the fact that, since criticism of collectivity and its structures were regarded as politically unsound, she and her co-workers has no immediate outlet for its expression. Incidents of crisis in collectives and cooperatives, sometimes leading to their collapse, were a frequent event in the 1970s when the concept of lesbian community was new and the hopes which it generated were unrealistically high. Few sources of psychological and practical assistance were available, since training in group interaction and the services of facilitators were scarce, particularly in the provinces. Today they are more readily available and, with women's emotional investment in the ideal of community better balanced, the situation has improved.

Dissatisfaction with lesbian community, as it was envisaged in the 1970s, did not result, fortunately, in women rejecting the concept outright. It prompted them to revise and modify it along more practical lines. By the mid-1980s lesbian community was starting to be seen less in terms of a homogeneous group of women with similar interests and attitudes than as a loose-knit assemblage in which differences of race, class, age and ideology are recognized and accepted. Black and working-class women made a significant contribution to this shift of perspective, by criticizing the racial and social narrowness and universalizing tendency which characterized the Lesbian Feminist Movement's concept of sisterhood.[47] This change in outlook was accompanied by a new mood of moderation which reflected the political conservatism of the age. It has resulted, sadly, in a decline in feminist commitment and activism. However, as Faderman comments, 'While the quest for Lesbian Nation had surely been lost, lesbianism as a lifestyle and the lesbian community were far from dead.'[48]

The fictional texts discussed below illustrate the different approaches to lesbian community which I have summarized. While they all concentrate attention on feminist groups and work-projects, their treatment of these topics varies according to the writer's ideological viewpoint and the attitudes of the period. The formal and stylistic features of the texts differ too. They range from the feminist realism of Piercy's *The High Cost of Living* to the utopian fantasy of Gearhart's *The Wanderground*. That Gearhart and other writers[49] should choose to employ the utopian mode as a vehicle for ideas of lesbian feminist community is understandable since the concept has, in fact, a distinct air of the utopian about it. As Nielsen wryly comments, contrasting the attraction which the ideal holds for women with its dream-like inaccessibility, 'We see community everywhere, in everything, but we seldom see it in detail. Like a mountain range on the horizon, it is most arresting at a distance.'[50]

The Wanderground is inspired by the concepts, popular with cultural feminists, of harmony between mind and body, universal sisterhood, and woman's affinity with nature. It is structured on an antithesis which is fundamental to feminist thought; this is 'the tension between the critique of an unsatisfactory present and the requirement, experienced as psychological or political, for some blueprint, however sketchy, of the future'.[51] The blueprint which Gearhart presents us with is, in fact, by no means sketchy. Certain features of it are familiar for, in creating it, she reworks the traditional pastoral motif of the dichotomy between the city and the country. The novel centres on the adventures of the Hill Women, a group of lesbian feminists who have migrated from the city to the countryside to establish a rural commune. Over the years they have developed powers of telepathy and telekinesis and now enjoy the ability to communicate with animals and birds. The intimate rapport which they enjoy with one another results in a representation of lesbian relations which, as well as being highly idealized, is, in my view, depicted in a manner which is sentimental and unconvincing. Misunderstandings and conflicts between the women appear rare, as are incidents of jealousy and rivalry. The harmonious nature of their life together stems partly from the fact that lesbian relationships are depicted in terms of woman-bonding, and little reference is made to their sexual aspect.

The Hill Women's decision to move from an urban to a rural environment is prompted, we are told, by the oppressive nature of city life. In juxtaposing the two areas, Gearhart draws a stark and simplistic contrast between the behaviour of the city dwellers, which in the case of both sexes is characterized by competition and violence, and the caring attitudes prevalent in the countryside. Urban culture is associated with male dominance and compulsory heterosexuality. Incidents of sexual harassment and rape are common, while laws have been instituted curtailing women's liberty and controlling their sexuality and style of dress. The novel also focuses attention on ecological issues, contrasting the city-dwellers' exploitative treatment of the environment with the Hill Women's enlightened approach. And the fact that the rural utopia which it depicts is multiracial in composition gives an opportunity to focus on issues relating to race.

An interesting feature of *The Wanderground* is that, unlike other examples of lesbian utopian fiction, it does not exclude male characters but attempts, albeit in a clumsy and unsatisfactory manner, to address the themes of male violence and the reconstruction of masculinity. The male figures portrayed are divided, somewhat schematically, into the categories of the macho residents of the city and the so-called 'Gentles' who, as their name implies, have successfully reconstituted their sexuality. The latter, though no doubt intended to represent a positive portrayal of masculinity, emerge as a feeble, lifeless group, devoid of energy and emotion. Influenced possibly by the negative attitude to male homosexuality manifested by some lesbian feminists,[52] Gearhart avoids portraying them engaging in gay relationships. Their lack of interest in sex helps to account for their general air of torpor.

A contradictory feature of *The Wanderground* is that, despite its over-romanticized image of rural life and cliché-ridden style, it has met with a notable degree of success and achieved, in fact, the status of a cult novel. An attribute which has no doubt contributed to this is its elaboration of the metaphorical term 'Lesbian Nation', which was extremely popular with lesbian feminists in the 1970s and 1980s. The concept of Lesbian Nation, while having its immediate source in Johnston's famous book,[53] also reflects other influences.[54] As a term for lesbian community it is, in some respects, misleading since it encourages lesbians to nurture hopes of achieving a degree of unity and separatism which are impractical. We do not belong to a single ethnic group or originate from a single geographical location. Nor – though we occasionally dream of this goal – do we speak a common language. However, the concept of Lesbian Nation, despite its lack of basis in fact, has had an empowering effect on women by providing a vivid image of lesbian identity and interaction. This is the function which it performs in *The Wanderground*. In associating urban culture with violence and death and portraying a group of women moving from the city to the country to start a new life together, Gearhart certainly has her finger on the pulse of lesbian culture and myth. In the 1970s, in both North America and the United Kingdom, a number of women did migrate from the city to the country to live in couples or communes.[55] And autobiographical accounts and stories produced by cultural feminists frequently locate lesbian feminist community in a rural setting. Several of the essays in *For Lesbians Only* display thematic affinities with the novel. One contributor describes how, wearying of withstanding incidents of harassment and attack in an urban environment, she decided to move to a rural one because, as she graphically puts it, 'i felt like i was dying internally, and that i was going to die, literally, if i continued to stay in the city.'[56] She joins a separatist farming commune and, while acknowledging the rigours of working on the land, like the Hill Women, values a rural lifestyle as an 'act of creating something new' and constructing 'a healthy environment for wimmin and the earth' (p. 253). Like them, moreover, she associates the city with violence and regards living in the country as conducive to developing one's 'psychic abilities' and encouraging 'a respect for the earth, a reverence for nature' (p. 256).

Very different from the idealized treatment of lesbian feminist community in *The Wanderground* is the complex and ambiguous representation which appears in the two other versions of lesbian pastoral discussed in this chapter, Piercy's *The High Cost of Living* and Anna Wilson's *Altogether Elsewhere*. Unlike Gearhart's novel, which uncritically reproduces the conventional pastoral dichotomy between city and country, Piercy's and Wilson's texts problematize and subvert it by foregrounding similarities between the two areas. They display other resemblances too. In concentrating attention on the activities of the lesbian feminist counterculture, they examine the strengths and weaknesses of organizations such as rape-crisis lines and women's support groups. Far from portraying lesbians as a unitary category, they acknowledge the existence of differences of class, race, intellectual interests and financial privilege. They also explore the tensions and conflicts to which these differences can give rise.

In recognizing the limitations of lesbian feminist community and concentrating attention on the theme of 'difference', Piercy is something of a pioneer, since in the mid-1970s when she wrote *The High Cost of Living*, a celebratory approach was in fashion and a focus on unity between women usual. The novel's treatment of class, like its analysis of sex, is unexpectedly radical. The protagonist Leslie, a graduate assistant at the University of Detroit, is portrayed as coming from an underprivileged background, and the struggle which she wages to gain a foothold in the middle-class world of the academy is precisely and painfully depicted. The imagery of blood and self-mutilation, which she employs in describing her effort to achieve upward mobility, highlights their self-destructive nature. As she sardonically remarks to her male friend Bernie, who like her is working-class and homosexual and is embarking on a similar ascent:

We're both wiggling upward, Bernie, we've shed our class. We've flayed ourselves bare and plastered over our bleeding flesh with accents and books and classes and everything we weren't and wanted to be.[57]

As this quotation illustrates, Leslie regards her academic aspirations with a strong degree of ambivalence. A key theme in the text is the conflict which she experiences between her allegiance to the lesbian feminist community and its values and her involvement in the heterosexist, male-dominated realm of the university. The former is represented by the group of women who, led by the indefatigable Tasha, run the local rape crisis-line, while the latter is epitomized by George, the Professor of History on whose patronage and tuition Leslie depends for economic survival and academic success. The cost of living, she discovers, is high in moral as well as financial terms. Despite the fact that she recognizes George's arrogance and capacity for ruthlessness, she ultimately chooses to throw in her lot with him and the ethic of capitalist competition which he represents. The novel concludes on a bitter note with her shamefacedly admitting that 'She wanted to live in Tasha's world only in her spare time' (p. 268) – and heading literally and metaphorically in George's direction.

Leslie's eventual capitulation to establishment values stems partly, the novel indicates, from the limitations of the various women's groups to which she has access and their failure, on account of their fragility and lack of intellectual sophistication, to understand the kind of conflicts which she is experiencing and give her support. Her fellow lesbians have little sympathy with her academic ambitions. They dismiss her research project of collating male-authored legal documents as colluding with patriarchy, failing to perceive that it will provide useful information about the social history of Detroit. She, in turn, dismisses the cultural feminist versions of women's history which they produce as mere 'old wives' tales' (p. 197). Her lack of rapport with them is illustrated by the fact that she chooses to divulge her problems not to them but to the male Bernie. Though irritated by his moodiness and egocentricity, she shares with him ties of class – and feels a greater affinity with him than with the women she knows. However, her relationship with Bernie does not run smoothly. One of the most original episodes in the novel is the incident in which, by taking advantage of her trust, he runs the risk of forfeiting her friendship for good. The fumbling sexual encounters which take place between the two are represented in a manner which is poignant as well as amusing. Here again the novel is ahead of its time. These episodes look forward to the focus placed by the lesbian sexual radicals on the contradictions and anomalies of sex and desire, and to the portrayal of gays and lesbians engaging in occasional sexual relations in Schulman's novels.[58]

Piercy's delineation of lesbian community is delicately balanced for, while exposing its shortcomings, she also acknowledges its positive features. She pays tribute to the strength and perseverance of the few women who, like Tasha, are genuinely committed to its ideals and who strive, in the face of appalling odds, to make them a practical reality. Her treatment of the topic is wide-ranging, introducing vignettes of rural life as well as urban. In juxtaposing the two areas, the novel creates an innovatory version of lesbian pastoral – one very different from *The Wanderground*. Lesbian life in the country is represented not as an undisturbed idyll but as marred by conflict and division. As Leslie perceives, on returning to Grand Rapids where she lived before moving to Detroit, the lesbian rural community is riven with animosities and jealousies stemming from differences of class and financial privilege. The feuds and inequalities which she witnesses prompt from her the angry comment, 'We're all supposed to be sisters, but they [women with private means] have more money and more control and more options, and they decide things to suit themselves' (p. 123).

The contradictory feelings which her encounter with country life provokes in Leslie are summed up in the observation: 'This was the only place where she had ever found acceptance as a lesbian, yet the narrowness of the world they had created grated on her nerves' (p. 119). It is one which those of us who live in the provinces or, due to the demands of our work, spend our lives travelling to and fro between the city and the country will probably endorse.

Altogether Elsewhere by the British Anna Wilson also concentrates attention on the theme of 'difference'. Like her previously published *Cactus* (1980),[59] *Altogether Elsewhere* questions the practicality of feminist community by highlighting the divisive effect of factors of class, age and material circumstances. Group-interaction and friction is a theme which Wilson treats with exceptional sensitivity and acumen, and the latter novel focuses on it even more strongly than the former. It is also more innovatory and adventurous from the point of view of style, exploring tensions and divisions between women in a narrative which is appropriately fractured and decentered.

In taking as its location the London Inner City, *Altogether Elsewhere* vividly evokes both the drabness and the menacing atmosphere of urban life. Capturing the mood of dereliction and despair which characterized Thatcher's Britain, the novel describes in a minimalist, rigorously honed-down style, 'decaying buildings, the city degenerating. Crushed waitresses leaning on smeared tables. People walking the streets without purpose.'[60] The narrative centres on a cluster of women who, though differing in race, class and sexual orientation, are temporarily brought together by a common desire to challenge male violence. Though 'conscious of being different, disparate', they none the less succeed in achieving brief 'acts of balance' with one another (p. 52). Under the leadership of the middle-aged Elsie, they transform themselves into a vigilante group and patrol the streets at night in pairs, with the aim of protecting women from rape and assault. Dehumanized by poverty and the monotony of their jobs, they strike the reader as, to a degree, anonymous. They communicate tersely in monosyllables, and are distinguishable chiefly by the distortions which manual labour has wrought on their physique or by signs of youth and age. Male violence is, on the whole, hinted at rather than described overtly. The threat which male sexuality poses is symbolically represented by the figure of the giant snowman which the boys build in the yard of the high-rise flats. The women, on approaching it, see 'vast genitals hang over them' (p. 36).

Wilson's delineation of the vigilante group and its activities, while affirming the value of feminist community, verges at times on the pessimistic. Emphasis is placed on the difficulties which the members, because of their different backgrounds and attitudes, experience in working together. Their motives for joining the group, when scrutinized closely, appear, in some cases, morally suspect. They reflect not only a desire for justice but also an element of sadism or a thirst for personal revenge. The effectiveness of the group as an instrument for challenging patriarchal power is also questioned. Elsie herself, in moments of depression, dismisses its activities as a mere 'subversive gesture', an example of 'anarchic foolishness' (p. 59).

The novel's predominantly urban location is occasionally punctured by episodes set on the coast or in the country. However, instead of employing these rural scenes to provide a contrast to and a respite from the dreary atmosphere of city life, Wilson utilizes them to highlight the all-pervasive influence of the patriarchal capitalist economy and its depressing effect on the psyche. Like Piercy, she problematizes the conventional dichotomy between city and country by alerting the reader to the fact that both areas form part of a single political system – one which oppresses women. Sitting on the promenade at a seaside resort gazing listlessly at the ocean, Gloria, a young black woman burdened with family cares, despondently perceives that 'She is not on holiday, after all. Wherever she goes, she must think the same thoughts' (p. 20).

Elsie's memories of working as a farm-hand in her youth are likewise depicted as the opposite of liberating. She mentally contrasts the optimistic cliché 'Take a breath of country air and forget your troubles' (p. 66), with the harsh reality of working on the land. Her memories of farm life consist not of tranquil landscapes but of 'dry, stubborn cows and bales too heavy to lift, and plodding home across the fields exhausted' (p. 67). Farming in the present age is premised, she recognizes, on 'a brutish simplicity' involving the ruthless exploitation and destruction of animals. It takes the form of 'draining cows of milk, of calves, finally of meat, their bodies shoved, impregnated, kicked, transported, sliced' (p. 67).

In representing the brutal nature of the capitalist consumer economy and its oppressive effects, Wilson draws a series of convincing analogies between ecological issues and sexual politics, by comparing acts of cruelty to animals with the male victimization of women. The connections which she makes between the two areas reveal thematic resemblances with Gearhart's *The Wanderground*. However, as my analysis of the two novels illustrates, these serve chiefly to spotlight their significant differences of viewpoint and perspective. Lesbian pastoral, as is the case with its mainstream counterpart, is multifaceted and displays a notable degree of diversity and flexibility. It employs a number of different narrative modes and is capable of articulating a variety of ideological positions and attitudes.

Writing lesbian fiction in a homophobic culture is arguably, by its very nature, a political enterprise. However, some kinds of lesbian fiction are more overtly political than others; the texts discussed in this chapter illustrate the varied forms of narrative created by writers who adopt an overtly political stance and who treat themes relating directly to sexual politics. A feature they share is the reworking of ideas from theoretical discourse. As well as highlighting the inventive treatment which these ideas receive, the texts also illustrate some of the problems which writers encounter in creating political fiction – and the strategies which they employ to negotiate and solve them.

The political implications of lesbian writing, as the texts considered above indicate, are something of a mixed blessing, revealing advantages and disadvantages. From a positive point of view, they give the writing of the text, whether a piece of fiction or theory, a sense of urgency and importance. On the negative side, however, by promoting the demand that writers create affirmative representations of lesbianism and exemplary role models, they may result, as in the case with Gearhart's *The Wanderground*, in depictions of lesbian relations which are over-idealized. The desire to emphasize the value of lesbian perspectives and relationships may also lead the writer to create prejudiced delineations of other sexual identifications. This is the case with the representation of female heterosexuality in Riley's *All That False Instruction*, and of bisexuality in Barbara Wilson's *Ambitious Women*.

However, though adopting an overtly political stance may involve the writer in difficulties, it can also result in the creation of lively and complex works. Certain of the novels discussed above, such as Piercy's *The High Cost of Living* and Anna Wilson's *Altogether Elsewhere*, illustrate this. They are intellectually innovative, and negotiate with a notable degree of success the problems which confront the writer who works in this area. In so doing, they give a new insight into lesbian feminist perspectives and into the complexities of women's life in a patriarchal culture.

Notes

1 Sarton, *A Reckoning* (Women's Press, 1984), p. 64.
2 Zimmerman, *The Safe Sea of Women*, ed. cit., p. 15.
3 Reina Lewis, 'The Death of the Author and the Resurrection of the Dyke', in *New Lesbian Criticism*, ed. cit., p. 17.

4 Ibid., p. 19.

5 Kaplan, 'Feminist Criticism Twenty Years On', in Helen Carr (ed.) *From My Guy to Sci Fi: Genre and Women's writing in the Postmodern World* (Pandora, 1989), p. 18. The essay claims to give an introduction to feminist criticism but Kaplan, while paying attention to other marginalized groups, ignores lesbian writing and criticism. The critic who most conspicuously ignores lesbian (and black) criticism and theory is Toril Moi (*Sexual/Textual Politics: Feminist Literary Theory*, Methuen 1985). Judith Roof gives an incisive critique of Moi and other feminist critics who devalue or contain lesbian and black critical perspectives in *A Lure of Knowledge: Lesbian Sexuality and Theory* (Columbia University Press, 1991), pp. 216–36.

6 Roller, *The Politics of the Feminist Novel* (Greenwood Press, 1986).

7 There is little reference to it in Mark Lilly (ed.) *Lesbian and Gay Writing: An Anthology of Critical Essays* (Macmillan, 1990).

8 Merck, *Perversions: Deviant Readings* (Virago, 1993), p. 7.

9 See Elizabeth Wilson, 'I'll Climb the Stairway to Heaven', ed. cit., pp. 191–4.

10 Zimmerman, *The Safe Sea of Women*, p. 16.

11 See Palmer, *Contemporary Women's Fiction*, ed. cit., pp. 7–8; and Rita Felski, *Beyond Feminist Aesthetics: Feminist Literature and Social Change* (Hutchinson, 1989), pp. 78–82.

12 Felski, op. cit., pp. 78–82, 152, 155, 161–2.

13 Zimmerman, *The Safe Sea of Women*, ed. cit., p. 25.

14 Zimmerman, *The Safe Sea of Women,* ed. cit., pp. 35–38.

15 See Elizabeth Wilson, 'I'll Climb the Stairway to Heaven', ed. cit., pp. 191–4; and Zimmerman, *The Safe Sea of Women*, ed. cit., pp. 35–8.

16 Felski makes a similar point about the feminist *bildungsroman* (op. cit., pp. 134–41).

17 Zimmerman, *The Safe Sea of Women*, pp. 36–69.

18 Examples include Roberts, *A Piece of the Night*, ed. cit.; Piercy, *The High Cost of Living* (Harper and Row, 1978); and Russ, *The Female Man*, ed. cit.

19 Elizabeth Wilson, 'I'll Climb the Stairway to Heaven', ed. cit., p. 193.

20 See note 18.

21 Radicalesbians, 'The Woman Identified Woman', ed. cit., p. 240.

22 Zimmerman, 'What Has Never Been', ed. cit., p. 178. For reference to Bunch and other theorists who focus on the lesbian's role as critic of patriarchal values, see Chapter 2, pp. 16, 21–22.

23 Riley, *All That False Instruction*, (Sirius Quality Paperback, 1981), p. 18.

24 Koedt, 'The Myth of the Vaginal Orgasm', ed. cit., pp. 198–207.

25 Sandy Boucher, 'Lesbian Artists', *Heresies*, 3 (1977), p. 43.

26 For reference to bisexuality, see Chapter 2, pp. 28–29.

27 Rich, 'Compulsory Heterosexuality and Lesbian Existence', ed. cit., pp. 51–68.

28 See Elizabeth Wilson, 'I'll Climb the Stairway to Heaven', ed. cit., pp. 187–8; and Modleski, *Feminism Without Women*, ed. cit., pp. 151–2.

29 Rich, 'Compulsory Heterosexuality and Lesbian Existence', ed. cit., p. 51.

30 Oosthuizen, *Loneliness and Other Lovers* (Sheba, 1981), p. 152.

31 'The Process of Writing Three Ply Yarn', in Elaine Hobby and Chris White (eds) *What Lesbians Do in Books* (Women's Press, 1991), pp. 239–55.

32 Sarah Franklin and Jackie Stacey discuss essentialist/constructionist approaches to lesbianism in 'Dyke Tactics for Difficult Times', in *Out the Other Side*, ed. cit., pp. 220–32.

33 March, *Three Ply Yarn* (Women's Press, 1986), p. 2. Subsequent references are to this edition and in the text.

34 For reference to the significance of race and ethnicity to lesbian culture and politics, see Faderman, *Odd Girls and Twilight Lovers*, ed. cit., pp. 285–89; and Zimmerman, *The Safe Sea of Women*, ed. cit., pp. 173–205.

35 See Zimmerman, *The Safe Sea of Women*, ed. cit., pp. 16–17.

36 See Felski, op. cit., pp. 96–8; and Suzanne Juhasz, 'Towards a Theory of Form in Feminist Autobiography: Kate Millett's *Flying* and *Sita*; Maxine Hong Kingston's *The Woman Warrior*', in Estelle C. Jelinek (ed.) *Women's Autobiography* (Indiana University Press, 1980), p. 237.

37 Faderman discusses the debates about pornography in *Odd Girls and Twilight Lovers*, ed. cit., pp. 249–58.

38 See the reference to Rich and Ryan in Chapter 2, pp. 19–20.

39 Burford, *The Threshing Floor* (Sheba, 1986), p. 112.

40 Bunch, 'Not for Lesbians Only', ed. cit., p. 68.

41 See Boucher, 'Lesbian Artists', ed. cit., p. 43; and Wittig, 'One is Not Born a Woman', (1981) in *The Straight Mind and Other Essays* (1992) pp. 15–20.

42 Elizabeth Wilson, 'I'll Climb the Stairway to Heaven', ed. cit., pp. 187–8; and Modleski, *Feminism Without Women*, ed. cit., p. 151.

43 Palmer, *Contemporary Women's Fiction*, ed. cit., pp. 62, 84, 115–17, 133–5.

44 Rich, *On Lies, Secrets and Silence: Selected Prose 1966–1978* (Virago, 1980), pp. 207, 213–14.

45 Faderman discusses these issues in *Odd Girls and Twilight Lovers*, ed. cit., pp. 230–35.

46 Nielsen, *Out the Other Side*, ed. cit., pp. 93–106.

47 See note 34.

48 Faderman, *Odd Girls and Twilight Lovers*, ed. cit., p. 279.

49 Examples include Katherine V. Forrest, *Daughters of a Coral Dawn* (Naiad, 1984); Anna Livia, *Bulldozer Rising* (Onlywomen, 1988); and Russ, *The Female Man,* ed. cit.

50 Nielsen, op. cit., p. 105.

51 Whitford, *Luce Irigaray:* ed. cit., p. 18.

52 See the discussion of Rich's ideas in Chapter 2, p. 20.

53 Johnston, *Lesbian Nation,* ed. cit.

54 Zimmerman discusses these in *The Safe Sea of Women*, ed. cit., pp. 121–6.

55 Faderman comments on this migration in *Odd Girls and Twilight Lovers*, ed. cit., pp. 238–40.

56 Iandras moontree, 'An Interview with a Separatist', in Hoagland and Penelope (eds) *For Lesbians Only*, ed. cit., pp. 252–3. See also Julia Penelope's fable 'A Cursory and Precursory History of Language', ibid., pp. 55–60.

57 Piercy, *The High Cost of Living*, ed. cit., p. 135.

58 See Schulman, *Girls, Visions and Everything* (Sheba, 1991), p. 143.

59 For critical discussion of Anna Wilson's *Cactus* see Palmer, *Contemporary Women's Fiction*, ed. cit., pp. 146–8.

60 Anna Wilson, *Altogether Elsewhere* (Onlywomen, 1985), p. 112.

4

Genre fiction: the thriller

It was just then that I jammed my hand into my jacket pocket and smashed my knuckles on a cold piece of metal. Then I remembered that I had a gun in my possession. I could use it any time I chose.
(Sarah Schulman *After Delores*, 1990: 27).

Genre fiction

The tendency of writers of lesbian fiction from the mid-eighties onwards to reject, temporarily at least, literary forms which are explicitly political in character, such as the Coming Out novel, and to experiment instead with reworking popular genres such as the thriller, science fiction and the comic novel, is not an isolated event. It forms part of the development of feminist genre fiction in general. The latter, which is likewise a product of the 1980s and 1990s, is controversial and has met with a mixed response. Champions of postmodern developments in literature, such as Helen Carr, welcome it on the grounds that a focus on genre results in a recognition of the diversity of women's fiction and an emphasis on the contract between reader and writer.[1] It also legitimizes the part played by pleasure and fantasy in reading and encourages writers to mingle high and low forms of culture, linking the mainstream with the marginal. Other critics, however, interpret the trend negatively. Patricia Duncker, who admits that the radical feminist slant of her study of contemporary feminist fiction *Sisters and Strangers* (1992) is 'out of step with the times',[2] expresses doubts about the value of genre fiction and feminist attempts to appropriate popular forms of writing. She argues that they entrap the writer in a network of conventions and reader-expectations which inhibit imagination and originality. She complains that 'All genre fiction is written with a market in mind' and 'operates within textual expectations which are indeed clichés' (Duncker 1992: 125).

In this instance I disagree with Duncker and the distinction which she makes. Genre fiction is not the only kind of writing which relies on conventions and re-employs ideas and motifs from earlier texts. Fiction which is overtly political in emphasis, as my discussion of the lesbian novels of the 1970s and the early 1980s illustrates, does too. As Carr rightly observes, 'All texts are dependent on and grow out of other texts' (Carr, 1989: 6). Moreover, the majority of writers work with a particular readership and market in mind. The radical feminist fiction of the 1970s, such as the novels of Piercy and Russ, would not have achieved the popularity and success which it did without the support of feminist publishers and a feminist readership.

A similar controversy revolves around lesbian experimentation in the field of genre. While some critics welcome it,[3] others express reservations.[4] In my opinion, though the revision of popular forms of fiction from a lesbian perspective may confront the writer with problems, its positive features outweigh the negative. Lesbian fiction is a marginalized form of writing and, until recently, has focused on a relatively narrow set of themes. The introduction of different genres, and the interplay of styles and conventions which this creates, enable it to achieve a greater degree of diversity. To approach lesbian fiction in terms of genre is also advantageous from a critical point of view. It promotes the recognition that, rather than there being a single text or canon of texts which reigns supreme and represents the pinnacle of lesbian writing, there is a variety of different kinds. Each serves a different purpose and has to be read in a different manner. Just as in the 1990s we no longer think in terms of a single lesbian identity but recognize differences of race, class and ideology between women, so too we appreciate differences of literary form and mode.

The writer's revision of popular genres, such as the thriller and the comic novel, is, in addition, intellectually and socially fruitful. It injects a fresh spark of vitality into her work and enables her to make contact with a wide range of readers. The clash and juxtaposition of different ideological perspectives which it generates can be politically challenging. As Duncker, despite her reservations about genre fiction in general, acknowledges, the lesbian rewriting of popular fictional forms is frequently 'subversive because the insertion of lesbian meanings into any kind of genre fiction disrupts the heterosexist codes of desire' (Duncker 1992: 99). This is the case with the texts discussed in the following two chapters. Exemplifying the thriller and the comic novel, two genres which have proved particularly popular with lesbians, they illustrate some of the strategies which writers employ in reworking conventions and motifs from the dominant culture. As well as offering a lively narrative, they interrogate and subvert hetero-patriarchal values and codes of conduct. The utilization of tactics of pleasure and play, which characterizes fiction of this kind, though representing a less direct and outspoken challenge to homophobic attitudes than that achieved by the overtly political fiction of the 1970s and early 1980s, is none the less transgressive in effect. Rather than adopting a tone of anger and using polemical methods, it employs strategies of entertainment to involve the reader in issues relating to sexual politics.

Contradictions, codes and conventions

As the debate which it has generated indicates, the incorporation of the thriller into the spectrum of contemporary lesbian writing is by no means unproblematic but reveals anomalies and contradictions. On the one hand, the format of the thriller holds attractions for the lesbian writer. It provides her with an effective vehicle for combining a focus on lesbian romance with the discussion of themes of interest to feminists. These, as is illustrated by the fiction of Rebecca O'Rourke, Mary Wings and other writers, include acts of violence perpetrated by men, the injustices and social abuses prevalent in contemporary society, and incidents of female victimization and resistance. The propensity of the thriller to focus on issues of a disturbing and controversial nature[5] is also an advantage. It encourages the writer of the lesbian thriller to address topics which, in the 1970s and 1980s, were avoided by certain sections of the Women's Movement on the grounds that they were contentious[6] or politically incorrect. The problematic aspects of collective organization which Barbara Wilson discusses;[7] women's capacity to commit acts of violence, treated by Katherine V. Forrest;[8] and sado-masochistic impulses and practices, explored by Schulman,[9] Wilson[10] and Wings,[11] are three such topics.

On the other hand, however, the format of the thriller and the values which it reflects can confront the writer with difficulties. The ideological attitudes associated with the genre constitute an obvious hurdle. The approach to class and sex in the detective fiction of Agatha Christie and Dorothy Sayers is, as critics point out,[12] elitist and puritanical. The values endorsed by male writers of crime fiction such as Mickey Spillane and Ian Fleming conflict even more strongly with lesbian/feminist attitudes. The works of these writers, as well as being misogynistic and often racist, tend to perpetuate a cult of male arrogance and individualism. The contradictions which the thriller displays in this respect are cogently summed up by Rosalind Coward and Linda Semple:

> In spite of the sympathetic, independent heroines and . . . the politically satisfying plots, the writers' acceptance of the individualistic and machismo codes of violence are highly problematic. It is highly problematic for feminists to replace the tough gun-toting man with a female equivalent and include little or no criticism of the violence of the Gumshoe novels.[13]

In discussing the figure of the investigator, Coward and Semple focus not only on the lesbian sleuth but also on her heterosexual counterpart portrayed in the novels of Sara Paretsky, Sue Grafton and Amanda Cross. Feminist thrillers and detective novels by these writers represent a subsection of the genre which is relevant to the work of lesbian writers. Lesbian and feminist forms of crime fiction, though differing in approach to sexual politics, reveal a number of common features. Both appropriate conventions and motifs from the work of mainstream writers, such as Christie and Raymond Chandler. They also share certain common topics, including the introduction of independent, resistant heroines, and a critique of patriarchal structures and male violence.

In addition to those mentioned above, there is another problem which confronts the writer who seeks to utilize the thriller to treat lesbian themes and interests. From the time of its inception in the early eighties the lesbian thriller has habitually introduced representations of sexual encounters and episodes focusing on romance. In fact, as I suggest in Chapter 6, at a time when many lesbian novels were depicting lesbian relationships in terms of woman–bonding and attachments of a primarily emotional kind, its frank and exuberant treatment of sex was one of its chief attractions for readers. However, in employing the thriller as a vehicle for treating sex and romance, the writer seeks to combine two genres which are, in fact, very different.[14] As Anna Wilson points out,[15] they carry different expectations of characterization and ideology. The protagonist of the romance (usually a woman) tends to display stereotypically 'feminine' affective attributes, such as emotional sensitivity, the willingness to cooperate, and responsiveness to the feelings of other people. The protagonist of the thriller, on the contrary, frequently a man, is portrayed as having typically 'masculine' instrumental qualities. These include powers of logic and deductive reasoning, along with a capacity for ruthlessness and aggression. In addition, he is generally represented as a loner. His methods of investigation are individualistic and he seeks to preserve his personal autonomy at all costs. Far from regarding romantic involvements and sexual encounters as the goal of life, as is the case with the protagonist of the romance, he sees them at the worst as a threat to his selfhood and at the best as a pleasurable, temporary distraction. It is interesting to note that, even in those thrillers where a romance narrative plays a key part, such as Sayers's Lord Peter Wimsey novels, obstacles preventing the protagonist's consummation and enjoyment of love are often introduced into the plot. As a consequence, s/he spends a considerable amount of time alone and is free to pursue her/his investigative activities unimpeded by the demands and interference of a partner.

Yet, though the characterization of the protagonist of the thriller is certainly at odds with that of her/his romance counterpart, the contrary attitudes which each embodies can, in fact, assist the writer of the lesbian thriller in creating the protagonist of her particular work. The figure of the lesbian, as constructed in contemporary culture, brings together attributes from both. The woman who identifies as lesbian struggles to maintain her autonomy in the face of homophobic pressures; like the protagonist of the thriller, she tends to be regarded by her heterosexual relatives and work-mates as an individualist and 'loner'. Simultaneously, however, she often seeks to become involved in the activities of the lesbian community and, like the protagonist of the romance, places value on love and sexual attach-ments. In fact, despite the role of loner assigned to her by the dominant culture, she herself frequently envisages her life as a quest for personal involvement and love. The question confronting the writer of the lesbian thriller is, how can she bring together these contrary interests and achieve a balance between them?

She Came in a Flash (1988) by the American Wings and *Death Wore a Diadem* (1989) by the Scottish Iona McGregor illustrate the kind of strat-egies which writers employ to integrate themes of sex and romance into the thriller format. They also give an insight into the way they combine fea-tures from the two different subsections of the genre – the detective novel and the crime novel.[16] The former, exemplified by the fiction of Christie, Sayers and Sir Arthur Conan Doyle, is characterized by an emphasis on the 'puzzle' element of the crime and a firm narrative closure, as well as by a conservative perspective and the use of an enclosed, often elitist, location. The latter, represented by the novels of Chandler and Dashiell Hammett, focuses on problems of a psychological nature and generally employs an urban setting. Though macho in attitude, it sometimes introduces percep-tions which are socially radical, exposing injustices in the legal and political system. In the lesbian thriller the categories of the detective novel and the crime novel, summarized above, seldom remain separate and distinct. The writer, while structuring her text primarily on one, frequently complicates and enriches its design by introducing features from the other. This is the course taken by Wings and McGregor.

She Came in a Flash is chiefly indebted to the conventions of crime fiction. Like Wings's previously published *She Came Too Late* (1986), to which it forms the sequel, it focuses on the adventures of the amateur sleuth, Emma Victor. Emma is articulate, fashion-conscious and exudes an air of glamour which is typically American in style. She is also, as her name implies, eminently successful in her investigative activities – though not always so in the realm of love. On this occasion it is the disappearance and subsequent murder of her old school friend Lana Flax, who has given up a career in science to join a Californian New Age commune, which prompts her to assume the role of investigator. The crime and its investigation are neatly constructed but, as is often the case in crime fiction, they take second place to interests of a social and psychological kind. The novel's central theme, which gives it a feminist interest and a polemical slant, is the analysis of the attractions which the cult of New Age therapy holds for women, along with a critique of its phony and dangerous aspects.

Wings's treatment of sex and romance is also indebted to the conventions of crime fiction. As is the case in Chandler's and Ian Fleming's novels, the women with whom the sleuth becomes sexually involved can be neatly divided into the contrary roles of 'villainess' and 'ally'. Bumper Lee, the ruthless crook at the centre of the murder plot, represents the former, while the disabled ballet dancer Roseanna, who works for the local women's community and gives Emma place of shelter when the going gets tough, plays the latter role. Emma's encounters with Bumper, it is interesting to note, are depicted as overtly sexual, while her relationship with Roseanna is more on the plane of woman-bonding. Again, as in the works of Chandler and Fleming, the villainess is portrayed as an alluring vamp while the ally is relegated to the role of pal. Emma's relationship with both women remains, on the whole, peripheral to the thriller story-line. This leaves her free to dominate the action and solve the murder mystery relatively single-handedly.

However, although *She Came in a Flash* is indebted to the conventions of crime fiction in general design, other features of its composition reflect the influence of the detective novel. The action takes place in the luxurious location of a Californian New Age Commune, a setting which resembles the enclosed, elitist milieu associated with the detective novel. The theme of conflict and competition between assertive, intelligent women, which the novel treats, also reflects detective novel conventions; it recalls episodes from the novels of Sayers and P.D. James.

McGregor's *Death Wore a Diadem* also displays an interplay of different genres. While the text is structured like a detective novel, McGregor's decision to set the story in nineteenth-century Edinburgh, combined with the references which she makes to women's contribution to the teaching and medical professions, link it to historical fiction. And the fact that she chooses as her focal location the Scottish Institute for the Education of the Daughters of Gentlefolk, a school catering for the education of aristocratic young girls, and makes a relationship between a pupil and teacher the central love interest, connects the novel to yet another genre – one with pronounced lesbian connotations. This is *fiction of the gynaeceum*.[17]

The novel, as suits its basis in the detective novel, has a complicated plot which centres on two puzzling events. A replica of a diadem belonging to the Empress Eugénie of France, who is due to pay a ceremonial visit to the Institute, mysteriously disappears from the building. Shortly afterwards Peggy Murdo, a housemaid at the Institute, is found murdered. A jewel from the diadem is discovered in the bag near her corpse, implicating her in the theft. The figure officially in charge of the crime investigation is James McLevy, ex-detective in the Edinburgh Police. His role, however, is quickly supplanted by Christabel MacKenzie, a pupil at the Institute. She is convinced of Peggy's innocence and, with the assistance of her lover Eleanor, a teacher, she investigates the crime and succeeds in clearing

Peggy's name. She also tracks down Peggy's killer and solves the mystery of the diadem's disappearance.

Death Wore a Diadem introduces a number of motifs commonly found in works of detective fiction. The ability of the intelligent amateur to surpass in investigative skills the official representative of the Police is one. It appears in the novels of Conan Doyle and Christie. The novel's plot structure reveals interesting affinities with Wilkie Collins's *The Moonstone* (1868). As in Collins's novel, the apparent theft of a piece of jewellery turns out not to be an act of theft in the conventional sense. The explanation for its disappearance lies in the field of psychology rather than crime detection.

The treatment of lesbian relationships in *Death Wore a Diadem* differs markedly from Wings's *She Came in a Flash*. Whereas in Wings's novel lesbian sex is represented by Emma's brief but sizzling romps with Bumper Lee, in McGregor's it takes the form of an involvement which, though sexual, is also emotional and romantic. This is in keeping with the representation of lesbian attachments in fiction of the gynaeceum, a genre which, as mentioned above, influences the text. In fact, in order to highlight the importance of Christabel's and Eleanor's relationship and integrate it into the fabric of the thriller storyline, McGregor transforms the crime investigation into a joint enterprise. The two women are portrayed working together to solve the mystery of the diadem's disappearance. This strategy, as well as emphasizing their emotional intimacy, rejects the solitary methods of investigation employed by male investigators and agents such as Dalgliesh, Marlowe and Bond, in exchange for a focus on feminist cooperation.

As the two novels of Wings and McGregor discussed above illustrate, the representation of personal relationships in lesbian crime fiction are extremely varied. They range from the romantic to the overtly sexual, introducing numerous gradations between the two. Yet another kind of involvement is depicted in Sandra Scoppettone's *Everything You Have is Mine* (1992). Here, the context of the crime investigation is the sleuth's stable, long-term relationship with her partner.

The focus on lesbian history, reflected in McGregor's *Death Wore a Diadem* in the locating of the relationship between Eleanor and Christabel in nineteenth-century Edinburgh and the delineation of their educational and professional activities, is also a feature of other works of lesbian crime fiction. Deborah Powell's *Bayou City Secrets* (1992) treats the lesbian past humorously. Placing the action in the Houston of the 1930s, Powell introduces a riproaring cast of gangsters, corrupt police officers and gold-digging whores. She also takes the opportunity to explore styles of lesbian behaviour from earlier eras, such as butch/femme role play. And in *Divine Victim* (Wings 1992), as we shall see, the portrayal of women from different generations allows Wings to contrast contemporary constructs of lesbianism with the liaisons and romantic friendships which existed in the past.

The investigator

The figure of the investigator, which is the hub of both the detective and the crime novel, poses significant difficulties for the writer of the lesbian thriller. The arrogant attitudes and ruthless methods of working which s/he frequently adopts are at odds with feminist principles of cooperation and noncoercion. Her/his role of independent loner conflicts with the ideals of feminist community. Moreover, the position of power and authority which many investigators, particularly the male ones, enjoy is inappropriate to the portrayal of the lesbian sleuth. The woman who identifies as lesbian, far from occupying a position of power and prestige, is likely to be stigmatized and socially marginal. She is a member of an oppressed minority group, and her way of life is regarded by the general public as dissident and transgressive. The role of investigator thus requires a degree of revision to become a suitable vehicle for the representation of lesbian characters and interests.

In remodelling the figure of the investigator to suit the circumstances of the contemporary lesbian and conform more closely with feminist attitudes, writers of the lesbian thriller employ a variety of different strategies. They emphasize the opportunity for observing people and events, and for assuming a disguise of anonymity, which the lesbian's marginalized position affords her. On occasion, they curb the attributes of self-sufficiency and power assigned to the sleuth in the traditional thriller and simultaneously introduce an element of feminist camaraderie into the plot by transforming the crime-investigation into a cooperative enterprise. Alternatively, they may problematize and deconstruct the investigator's role by highlighting its contradictions and foregrounding the risks and dangers which it involves. Another strategy which writers employ is to undermine the power traditionally assigned to the sleuth by linking her role to that of the victim of the crime – or even, in some texts, its perpetrator. I intend to explore these strategies and discuss some of the effects to which they give rise.

McGregor's *Death Wore a Diadem*, as illustrated above, employs the second of these strategies. It transforms the crime-investigation into a cooperative enterprise. Another novel which takes a similar course is Barbara Wilson's *Murder in the Collective* (1984). The narrative centres on a sudden outbreak of crime in two collective business organizations: the mixed Best Printing and the lesbian separatist B. Violet Typesetting. Pam Nilsen, who works for the former, joins forces with Hadley, a member of the latter, and the two women investigate the crime together.

The concept of a joint investigation, as well as introducing an element of feminist cooperation into the plot, also furthers the interests of lesbian romance. Romance is of key importance in *Murder in the Collective* since, as well as being a thriller, it is also a Coming Out novel. In the course of their investigative partnership Pam, who previously identified as heterosexual, falls in love with Hadley – and the two embark on an affair. In the first half of the novel, episodes focusing on crime investigation interact smoothly with those treating love and romance. In the second half, however, the tension which exists between the genres of the thriller and the romance becomes apparent. The feat of solving the crimes in the two collectives, which Pam and Hadley achieve together, ironically results in the break-up of their relationship. While interrogating suspects, Hadley happens to re-encounter Fran, an old flame. Fran is an alcoholic, and Hadley, deciding that she needs her help, breaks off the relationship with Pam and goes back to her. Pam thus returns to the position of 'loner', traditionally assigned to the figure of the investigator, which she occupied in the opening pages. This leaves her free to embark on other investigations and become involved in further romantic liaisons in subsequent novels.

Another strategy, which writers of the lesbian thriller employ to modify and adapt the conventional role of the investigator, is to focus attention on its contradictions. They intersperse references to the power and prestige which the sleuth enjoys with those highlighting the dangerous and pre-carious aspects of the role. The fact that the sleuth in the lesbian thriller is a woman, lacks the protection of a man, and often operates in an urban environment, allows ample opportunity for the use of this device. It has the additional advantage of forging a link between the protagonist and the female reader by assigning to the former emotions and perceptions with which the latter can easily identify. Wings makes effective use of this strategy in *She Came Too Late*. Having convinced the reader of Emma Victor's courage and quick-wittedness by portraying her engaging in some outrageously daring adventure, she suddenly punctures her 'superwoman' image and unexpectedly returns her to the level of 'everywoman'. She reminds us that, like the rest of us, Emma experiences city life as dangerous and scary. In one particular episode Emma inserts her ring of keys between her fingers and positions them as a weapon of defence.[18] In another, she describes herself as playing what she humorously calls 'the Women's Safety Game' and takes a series of simple precautions to avoid attack (Wings 1986: 171). These increase reader identification and give Emma's adven-tures a firm material and social base, lending them authenticity and realism. They also have the effect of temporarily transforming the novel into a woman's safety manual by giving the reader some useful tips on self-defence and street-wise behaviour. An attractive feature of the lesbian thriller, one which helps to account for its popularity, is the practical information about social life which some texts give the reader. In so doing, they conform to thriller and romance conventions. Chandler comments on the propensity of thriller writers to introduce references to 'clothes by Vogue and decor by House Beautiful'[19] into their novels. The most famous exponent of this trend is, of course, Fleming who, in his James Bond novels, gives detailed descriptions of sartorial fashion, drinks and haute cuisine. Following his example, Wings offers the reader detailed

descriptions of fashion and cuisine. However, unlike him, she intersperses
reference to these frivolous topics with tips on the serious matter of female
safety.[20]

A more drastic strategy which writers of the lesbian thriller employ to
undermine the investigator's pretensions to power and to problematize the
attributes of arrogance and self-sufficiency, which the role embodies, is to
portray her as a naive persona and an object of humorous ridicule. Barbara
Wilson's *Sisters of the Road* (1987) makes fruitful use of this device. Wilson
cleverly develops and exaggerates the qualities of fallibility and insecurity
which are features of the sleuth's character in certain works of American
crime fiction.[21] At the start of the novel Pam Nilsen, again cast in the role
of investigator, behaves in the arrogant, high-handed manner reminiscent
of the male investigator in the traditional thriller. As the narrative progresses, however, her pretensions to authority and independence are punctured and deflated. A tension is established between the conventional way
in which Pam envisages the narrative unfolding in her imagination, with
herself dominating the action and her colleague Carole playing the subordinate roles of side-kick and girl-friend, and the less glamorous and successful
scenario which actually occurs.

One of the most inventive strategies which writers of the lesbian thriller
employ to quality and interrogate the attributes of power and authority
assigned to the figure of the investigator, is to portray her not in the
conventional role of dynamic agent who dominates the action but in the
role of victim. This device gives rise to diverse effects. It is utilized by
the British O'Rourke, who introduces elements of pathos and vulnerability
into the characterization of the sleuth, and by the American Schulman who
establishes a complex web of connections linking the investigator to the
murder victim.

In *Jumping the Cracks* (1987) O'Rourke develops the qualities of solitariness
and personal insecurity manifested by certain investigators in American crime
fiction, such as Chandler's Marlowe, to represent the feelings of loneliness,
uncertainty and alienation which the woman who identifies as lesbian frequently experiences in contemporary society. Living alone in London, where
she survives on social security and occasional spells of casual work, the
investigator Rats exemplifies the depressing aspects of lesbian urban existence. She is sullen and uncommunicative in her relations with employers
and acquaintances, hiding her lesbianism under a defensive mask. Like the
investigator in the American crime novel, she conceals attributes of intelligence and perception beneath a taciturn persona. Her isolated situation and
precarious financial position make her an obvious target for persecution –
one which the villain Pershing is quick to exploit. *Jumping the Cracks* is,
however, a story of lesbian survival, not defeat. Rats epitomizes, in fact, the
contradictions of vulnerability and strength, impotence and power, which
characterize the portrayal of the lesbian sleuth and help explain the attraction

which she holds for female readers. Rats's negative features and air of pathos are offset by, and serve to highlight, her positive qualities of tenacity and intelligence. These enable her to resist Pershing's attempts at intimidation and eventually solve, single-handedly, the mystery of the corpse which she glimpsed dumped on the passenger seat of a parked car.

In order to emphasize Rats's courage and independence, and to give her a free hand in solving the murder mystery, O'Rourke keeps the romance narrative which is a feature of the novel relatively separate from the thriller storyline. Rats's lover Helen, though initially helping her in the murder investigation, eventually loses faith in it. She dismisses Rats's efforts to discover the identities of the corpse and its killer as futile. For much of the novel the two characters remain apart and have little contact. This enables Rats to maintain the role of independent loner which the sleuth traditionally occupies.

Schulman's *After Delores* (1988) develops the emphasis on the sleuth's pathos and vulnerability, taking it to unprecedented extremes. Challenging the assumption common to the majority of thrillers, that the positions of the investigator and the victim of the crime are poles apart, she creates a network of connections and affinities linking the two figures.

Nobody could differ more radically from the conventional model of the investigator than the nameless narrator turned sleuth whose subjectivity Schulman's novel explores. A waitress in a New York cafe, whose depressive tendency to 'think about sad things'[22] is speedily driving her to alcoholism, she is, at the start of the novel, preoccupied with matters very different from crime detection. She is consumed with feelings of rage and jealousy at her betrayal by her lover Delores who has jilted her for another woman. As this scenario suggests, the novel owes more to the conventions of the romance than the thriller. Indicative of this is the fact that the narrator assumes the role of sleuth by accident rather than by design; her investigative activities are motivated by passion not reason. On hearing that her friend Marianne Walker, whom she nicknames Punkette, has been murdered, she transfers onto the circumstances of her death the anger and obsessive desire for vengeance which she feels toward Delores. The role of the investigator and the gun in her possession which symbolizes it, confer on her an unaccustomed sense of power. They enable her temporarily to transcend the attacks of despair and paranoia to which she is prone.

There is another motive which prompts the narrator to adopt the role of sleuth and track down Punkette's killer. This is the ambiguous emotional response which she feels toward her. She is sexually attracted to Punkette and, at the same time, identifies with her. She sees Punkette and herself as victims of a gross injustice. They have both put their trust in love – and found it betrayed.

Schulman introduces a number of different devices to emphasize the identification between the two characters. The gun, which the narrator originally intended to use to revenge herself on Delores, becomes the weapon which she uses to avenge Punkette's murder. Fantasies of wreaking vengeance on Delores (smashing her face with a hammer or bashing it in) blur disturbingly with fantasies of shooting Punkette's killer. Many of the experiences which the narrator undergoes in investigating the murder take the form of an uncanny repetition of Punkette's. Like Punkette, she encounters the exotic actress Charlotte and becomes for a time infatuated with her. Like Punkette, she becomes involved in an intricate triangular relationship with Charlotte and her lover Beatriz.

By establishing a sense of identification between the narrator and Punkette, Schulman achieves several different goals. She problematizes and deconstructs the conventional role of investigator, demonstrating the inappropriateness of the attributes of authority, rationality and independence which s/he traditionally displays, particularly in relation to the position of the working-class lesbian. The latter's position, Schulman suggests, in the respect that she is stigmatized, socially marginal and financially deprived, has more in common with the victim of the crime than with the investigator.

Schulman also perceptively delineates the complexities and contradictions of lesbian love. Her portrayal of the narrator's ambiguous involvement with Punkette illustrates the fact that, as Butler points out,[23] a frequent feature of lesbian relationships, one that challenges a psychoanalytic assumption that identification and desire are mutually exclusive, is that the female subject may feel attracted to another woman while simultaneously identifying with her. *After Delores* subtly explores the psychological process of the coexistence of identification and desire.

Whereas Schulman challenges convention by establishing affinities between the investigator and the victim of the crime and weaving threads of identification linking the two figures, other writers make connections between the investigator and the criminal. Kate Delafield, the sleuth in Forrest's *Murder at the Nightwood Bar* (1987), is portrayed as a member of the Los Angeles Police and exemplifies that most contradictory and problematic of characters – the lesbian cop. The conflicts and tensions of her role, trapped as she is between the establishment world of the Police Force and the transgressive world of lesbian involvements, come to a head when she is required to investigate the murder of a member of the local lesbian club. While interrogating a male suspect, she unwisely allows 'her rage as a lesbian woman'[24] to get the better of her professional self-control. She is so angered by his homophobic taunts that she loses her cool and attacks him. This violent outburst links her, in the reader's mind, to the figure of the murderer who, in this novel, is represented as female. The linking of the two figures has the effect of breaking down the clear-cut division between sleuth and criminal, which is a characteristic of the traditional thriller, and highlighting the equivocal and liminal position which the lesbian occupies in society. While Kate's connections with the Police align her with the forces of law and order, her unorthodox sexual orientation makes her a social outlaw and dissident.

Wings's *Divine Victim* develops the strategies described above by taking the unusual step of linking the figure of the investigator to both the victim of the crime and the criminal. The novel also illustrates the practice of combining different genres, which is a feature of contemporary women's fiction in general[25] and, as is illustrated by some of the texts discussed in this chapter, the lesbian thriller in particular.

In focusing on sexual attachments between women from an earlier generation as well as those living in the present age, and juxtaposing episodes set in different periods, *Divine Victim* reveals links with historical fiction. It also has pronounced Gothic resonances. In fact, as is signalled by the name of the deceased woman whose mystery the sleuth seeks to unravel and by the allusion to Manderley introduced in the opening pages, the text reworks, from a lesbian viewpoint, episodes from Daphne DuMaurier's famous Gothic romance *Rebecca* (1938).[26] The publication of Wings's novel is, in this respect, apposite since it occurs around the same time as that of Margaret Forster's biography of DuMaurier which explores the latter's erotic involvements with women.

Wings interrelates the different genres in which she works with relative skill. Taking her cue from writers such as Conan Doyle and, in the field of the lesbian thriller, Vicki P. McConnell,[27] she establishes an interplay between the conventions of the thriller and certain Gothic themes and motifs. The latter include the flight of a cloaked female figure into the night, with which the novel opens; the reference to a valuable heirloom concealed in an ancestral mansion; the interaction of allusions to sacred and profane love; and the representation of the convent as a place of female entrapment. The revelation that the investigator, while herself a victim of attack, has in the past participated in a murder, though certainly unexpected, reflects the ambiguous role which is traditionally assigned to the heroine of Gothic romance.[28] She is portrayed simultaneously as an innocent victim of persecution and a resolute survivor who, as Wings intimates, is capable of perpetrating an act of violence when her safety so requires.

Rather than treating these motifs entirely seriously, Wings introduces an element of comic pastiche. The predictable romance plot, and the search for the hidden heirloom which forms its basis, are playfully parodied and undercut.

Divine Victim also illustrates a feature of the lesbian thriller which I mentioned at the start of this chapter. This is the licence which the genre gives the writer to explore topics which other kinds of fiction avoid treating because they are regarded as politically incorrect or 'taboo'. Roberts, criticizing the idealized representation of characters and relationships which occurs in many lesbian novels, humorously remarks, 'I'd like to read a romance about a lesbian sadist!'[29] If she turns to the episodes in Wings's novel which treat the narrator's tempestuous involvement with the art historian Ilona Jorgensen, she will find her wish fulfilled, with comic exaggeration. Manipulative, sadistic and self-obsessed, Ilona could be seen as a nightmarish image of that misogynistic cliché of phallocentric culture – the lesbian as monster. However, by contrasting her with other more agreeable lesbian characters, Wings avoids the trap of misogyny. One may criticize her portrayal of Ilona on the grounds that it is sensational and panders to the current fascination with SM. However, in my opinion, its effect is harmless – even, possibly, therapeutic. It liberates the reader, by giving her permission to confront the negative aspects of lesbian relationships which, in the 1970s and 1980s, many of us felt too inhibited to discuss – let alone write about! The fact that writers such as Wings, Schulman and DeLynn are starting to explore imbalances of power between women in their fiction is a sign of a new openness. It also illustrates the confidence which they feel in their literary abilities and in a more mature gay audience.

Notes

1 Carr, 'Introduction', *From My Guy to Sci Fi*, ed. cit., pp. 5–10.
2 *Sisters and Strangers* (Blackwell, 1992), p. 260.
3 See Maggie Humm, *Border Traffic: Strategies of Contemporary Women's Fiction* (Manchester University Press, 1991), pp. 194–200; and Munt, 'The Inverstigators: Lesbian Crime Fiction', in Susannah Radstone (ed.) *Sweet Dreams: Sexuality, Gender and Popular Fiction* (Lawrence and Wishart, 1988), pp. 91–119.
4 See Anna Wilson, 'Lesbian Gumshoes', *Bay Windows* 6(7) (18–24 February 1988), pp. 1–2; and Zimmerman, *The Safe Sea of Women*, ed. cit., pp. 211–12.
5 Examples include incest (P.D. James, *Devices and Desires*, Faber, 1989); sexual violence (John Harvey, *Lonely Hearts*, Viking, 1989); and prostitution (Ruth Rendell, *A Demon in my View*, Hutchinson, 1976).
6 I explore the treatment of such topics in the lesbian thriller in my discussion of 'Fiction of Debate' in 'The Lesbian Thriller: Crimes, Clues and Contradictions', in Gabriele Griffin (ed.) *Outwrite: Lesbianism and Popular Culture* (Pluto, 1993).
7 Barbara Wilson, *Murder in the Collective* (Women's Press, 1984).
8 Forrest, *Murder at the Nightwood Bar* (Pandora, 1987).
9 Schulman, *After Delores*, ed. cit.
10 Barbara Wilson, *The Dog Collar Murders* (Virago, 1989).
11 Wings, *Divine Victim* (Women's Press, 1992).
12 Cora Kaplan, 'An Unsuitable Genre for a Feminist?', *Women's Review*, 8 (1986), pp. 18–19.
13 Coward and Semple, 'Tracking Down the Past: Women and Detective Fiction', in *From My Guy to Sci Fi*, ed. cit., p. 46.
14 For reference to the romance and its conventions see Jean Radford (ed.), *The Progress of Romance: The Politics of Popular Fiction* (Routledge and Kegan Paul,

1986); and Janice A. Radway, *Reading the Romance: Women, Patriarchy and Popular Literature* (University of North Carolina Press, 1984).

15 'Investigating Romance: Who Killed the Detective's Lover?', paper given at the Fifth Annual Lesbian and Gay Studies Conference, Rutgers University, New Brunswick, NJ, 1–3 November 1991.

16 See Julian Symons, *Bloody Murder: From the Detective Story to the Crime Novel: A History* (Penguin, 1972), pp. 162–4; and Gerry Palmer, *Thrillers: Genesis and Structure of a Popular Genre* (Edward Arnold, 1978), pp. 40–52.

17 For reference to this genre, see Elaine Marks and George Stambolian, *Homosexualities and French Literature: Cultural Contexts/Critical Texts* (Cornell University Press, 1979), pp. 353–77; and Gill Frith, *The Intimacy which is Knowledge: Female Friendship in the Novels of Women Writers*, PhD dissertation, University of Warwick, 1989, pp. 304–35. See also Paulina Palmer, 'Antonia White's *Frost in May*: A Lesbian Feminist Reading', in Susan Sellers (ed.) *Feminist Criticism: Theory and Practice* (Harvester Wheatsheaf, 1991), pp. 89–108.

18 Wings, *She Came Too Late*, ed. cit., p. 171.

19 Chandler, 'The Simple Art of Murder', reprinted in *Pearls Are a Nuisance* (Penguin, 1964), p. 190.

20 Barbara Wilson's *Sisters of the Road* (Women's Press, 1987, pp. 47–8) also gives the reader information about city life.

21 See Stephen Knight, '"A Hard Cheerfulness": An Introduction to Raymond Chandler', in Brian Docherty (ed.) *American Crime Fiction* (Macmillan, 1988), pp. 80–2.

22 Schulman, *After Delores,* ed. cit., p. 9.

23 Butler, 'Imitation and Gender Insubordination', ed. cit., p. 26.

24 Forrest, *Murder at the Nightwood Bar,* ed. cit., p. 109.

25 Examples include novels by Margaret Atwood and Angela Carter.

26 Wings discussed Gothic fiction in her paper 'Lesbian Gothics – Victim or Victor?' at the 'Activating Theory' Conference, University of York, 9–11 October 1992.

27 See Conan Doyle, *The Hound of the Baskervilles* (Newnes, 1902); and McConnell, *Mrs Porter's Letter* (Naiad, 1982) and *The Burnton Widows* (Naiad, 1984).

28 See Juliann E. Fleenor (ed.) *The Female Gothic* (Eden Press, 1983), pp. 3–28.

29 'Write, she said', in *The Progress of Romance*, ed. cit., p. 231.

5

Genre fiction:
the comic novel

Carnivalistic laughter is directed toward something higher − toward a
shift of authorities and truths, a shift of world orders. Laughter embraces
both poles of change, it deals with the very process of change, with *crisis*
itself.

(Mikhail Bakhtin 1984: 127)

Comedy, satire, laughter

A role frequently assigned to the lesbian by contemporary theorists is critic
and 'disruptor'[1] of heterosexuality. Whether arguing that heterosexuality is
an institution as Rich does,[2] questioning its sexual categories like Wittig,[3]
or illustrating its 'constructed status'[4] like Butler, the lesbian seeks to problematize and challenge heterosexual norms and conventions. Writers of
fiction also contribute to this role. In exposing the injustices and contradictions in heterosexual codes of conduct and systems of thought, some, such
as Piercy and Riley, employ, as we have seen, directly political methods
involving polemic. Writing in the realist mode, they encourage the reader
to identify with the protagonist's oppressed position and share her feelings
of outrage and distress at the incidents of bigotry and prejudice which she
encounters. Others, such as Russ and Livia, whose novels are discussed in
this chapter, employ subtler strategies. Puncturing the realist veneer of their
texts with surreal episodes and passages of authorial address, they introduce
humorous and ironic perceptions. The humour which informs their novels
is often satiric. It creates the kind of comedy which, to quote Judy Little,
'mocks the norm radically' and 'manifests the distinctive features of inversion, mocked hierarchies and . . . redefinitions of sex identity'.[5] Lesbianism
is celebrated as a liberating, transgressive phenomenon which destabilizes
and puts in question conventional models of sexual relations, along with the
heterosexual matrix which forms their base.

The lesbian comic novel, unlike other kinds of lesbian genre fiction such

'9 out of 10 cats' by Cath Jackson (1988)

'I've rung Lesbian Line' by Angela Spark and Cath Tate (1988)

British artists protest at Section 28 (Cartoons produced by permission of Cath Jackson and Cath Tate)

as the thriller and science fiction, has received, up to now, little critical attention. Indicative of this is the fact that reviewers and critics, when discussing Winterson's *Oranges Are Not the Only Fruit*, generally treat the novel in isolation and write as if its subversive style of humour is unprecedented.[6] This, in fact, is not the case. The comic scenarios which Winterson creates, inventive though they are, develop a tradition of lesbian humour which, having originated in the 1970s, has increased in wit and sophistication and finds expression in the 1980s and 1990s in a variety of cultural forms – theatrical, artistic and literary. Examples include the performances of the Split Britches Cabaret;[7] the stunts performed by the Queer Activist groups ACT UP and OutRage;[8] and the series of graphics and cartoons produced by Cath Jackson, Angela Spark and Cath Tate. The latter, as well as ridiculing and parodying heterosexual conventions, launch a protest at the anti-gay legislation contained in Section 28.[9] Among writers who contribute to this tradition are the Americans June Arnold and Russ, the British Livia and the Indian Namjoshi. Their texts are intellectually and stylistically innovative.

Following the development of the discourses of psychology and psychoanalysis, much has been written about the disruptive and liberatory effects of laughter. Hélène Cixous, challenging the traditional representation of the Medusa as a monster and portraying her as a source of creative inspiration, remarks, 'She's not deadly. She's beautiful and she's laughing.'[10] Kristeva, discussing the subversive significance of laughter, argues that it 'lifts inhibitions by breaking through prohibitions . . . to introduce the aggressive, violent, liberating drive'.[11] This is the function which laughter performs in the works of fiction discussed below. Guffaws erupt not only from the reader enjoying them but also from the characters which they portray. Esther, the university lecturer represented in Russ's *On Strike Against God* (1980), is haunted by the ghost of a male psychoanalyst whose clinic she once attended. He materializes in the guise of Count Dracula and, baring his fangs, accuses her of being a man-hater and suffering from penis envy. Having put up with his taunts for some minutes, Esther decides that she has had enough. She is perfectly capable, she tells us, of taming her 'interior monsters'.[12] She exorcises him, and the anxieties which he arouses, with an irreverent burst of laughter: 'Snoork! I laugh.' (Russ 1987: 9)

This episode from Russ's novel, like others in the texts considered below, is carnivalesque in mood. By ridiculing a male authority figure who is a spokesman for phallocentric values, it inverts the perspectives of the dominant culture and creates, to quote Bakhtin, 'a world inside out'. Esther's subversive laughter has the effect of 'liberating us from the prevailing point of view of the world, from conventions and established truths' and 'offers us the chance to have a new outlook'.[13]

Feminists, particularly those who identify as lesbian, are not noted for their sense of humour. On the contrary, they are often dismissed by the general public as a puritanical, strait-laced bunch. One of the insults which Esther encounters from her male academic colleagues is the accusation that, like all 'women libbers', she is over-sensitive and incapable of seeing a joke (p. 31). The role of woman humorist, as this suggests, is a relatively new one and is beset with contradictions. On the one hand, she writes from the margins, occupies a subordinate role in society and is frequently at odds with the values of the dominant culture. On the other, she seeks to occupy the privileged position of satirist and public truth-teller.[14] The tension between power and powerlessness, which informs women's humorous writing in general, is magnified in lesbian writing. The lesbian viewpoint, as Sandy Boucher convincingly argues, creates an 'extra dimension', one which 'puts us a step outside of so-called normal life and lets us see how gruesomely abnormal it is'. It gives rise, she claims, to a 'world-view that is distinct in history and uniquely liberating'.[15]

Yet for the lesbian writer to achieve the confidence to utilize and exploit this perspective and 'world view', employing them to create a critique of heterosexist values and attitudes, is by no means easy. This is illustrated by the fact that only with the advent of the Lesbian Feminist Movement in the 1970s has lesbian comic fiction emerged and developed into a specific literary genre. It appears to be the Movement, and the communal support it provides, which has given the writer the strength and sense of group support to create fiction of this kind. It also, of course, provides a readership for the texts which she produces. Themes such as Coming Out, the incidents of prejudice and discrimination which lesbians encounter, and the pleasures and disappointments of lesbian social life play a key part in lesbian comic novels. They are familiar to the majority of us, and the writer relies on them to form a bond between herself and her readers. This bond provides the foundation for the problematization of heterosexuality, and the delineation of the pitfalls and absurdities of lesbian existence in contemporary 'straight' culture in the texts discussed below.

Problematizing heterosexuality

One of the earliest and best-known examples of lesbian comic fiction is Rita Mae Brown's *Ruby Fruit Jungle* (1973). A *bildungsroman* written in the confessional style popular in the 1970s, it recounts in a breezy, colloquial tone the adventures of the narrator Molly Bolt. Focus is placed on Molly's childhood in Pennsylvania, her years at college and, most important of all, her discovery of her lesbian orientation. *Ruby Fruit Jungle* achieved the status of a cult work in the newly-formed lesbian groups of the period and is generally remembered for its exuberantly frank celebration of lesbian sex. However, in the heterosexist climate of the early 1970s, this celebration could not take place without careful preparation on the author's part. In

order to make a space for it and render it convincing, Brown first has to
problematize heterosexual attitudes and values. She carries out this task
with wit and panache.

A key feature of *Ruby Fruit Jungle* is the humorous critique which it gives
of romantic love and the importance which society attaches to heterosexual
relations. Brown's treatment of these topics agrees with the radical feminist
perspectives of Koedt and Millett, theorists who interrogate codes of romantic love and criticize society's fetishing of sexual intercourse. Brown
treats these issues in a manner which is playfully iconoclastic. Teenager
Connie, regaling Molly and her other girl friends with an account of her
first experience of sex with a man, rejects the romantic notion that intercourse is 'a beautiful experience . . . the most intimate experience a human
being can have'.[16] Concentrating instead on its mundane and ridiculous
aspects, she describes the prelude to the sex act as 'a half hour of dry
humping and rolling all over the bed' (Brown 1978: 79). As for the act
itself, she laconically remarks that it is 'okay, but I can't believe that they
write songs about first times and people kill themselves over it. I mean
really!' (p. 80) Other episodes in the novel develop this critique. The
female characters complain about the 'messy' and uncomfortable aspects of
hetero sex (p. 100) and ridicule male sexual inhibitions (p. 70). One of
them discovers to her astonishment that she prefers sex with women to sex
with men – and insists on giving Molly what she calls 'kissing lessons' to
demonstrate the fact! (p. 102)

Episodes such as this, which problematize heterosexual practice and its
supposed pleasures, are interspersed with others which expose the oppressive effects of gender stereotyping and inequalities between the sexes.
Young Molly's announcement that she intends to be a doctor when she
grows up is greeted with ridicule by the other children: 'You can't be a
doctor. Only boys can be doctors' (p. 31). Confusions and *non sequiturs*
about sexual identity and gender difference are also subjected to playful
scrutiny. Leroy, one of Molly's male friends, interprets her decision to
purchase a motor bike as evidence that she is 'queer'. Revealing his insec-
urities about his masculinity, he plaintively protests, 'If you're doing what
you please out there riding around on your motor-cycles, then what am I
supposed to do? I mean how do I know how to act if you act the same
way?' (p. 63). The humour of these gender-bending episodes is enhanced
by the fact that both Molly and Leroy turn out to be gay.

The themes treated in *Ruby Fruit Jungle* recur, frequently in a more
complex and sophisticated form, in the works of lesbian comic fiction
published subsequently. The problematization of heterosexual sex, and the
exposé of the social pressures imposed on women to recruit them into
relations with men, continue to play a significant part in the fiction of the
1980s, though they are generally treated in a less simplistic and one-sided
manner. The texts published in the 1980s, rejecting the lesbian chauvinism

of the previous decade and the message it promoted that all lesbian practices are good and all heterosexual ones bad, generally accompany their critique of heterosexuality with a reference to the problematic aspects of lesbian relations or the contradictions of sex and desire in general. Russ's *On Strike Against God* questions the assumption, encouraged by the 1960s Sexual Revolution, that women have to be sexually active and invariably enjoy sex with men. The narrator Esther tersely observes, 'the truth that's never told today about sex is that you aren't good at it, that you don't like it, that you haven't got much. That you're at sea and unhappy' (Russ 1987: 9). The novel, however, balances this negative representation of heterosexuality with an emphasis on the difficulties which lesbian relationships can involve. Esther's description of her first experience of making love with a woman (her colleague Jean), while warmly tender and affirmative, acknowledges the anxieties and feelings of insecurity which, on account of their frequently closeted nature and lack of social recognition, lesbian involvements sometimes reveal (pp. 52–58).

Livia's *Relatively Norma* (1982), a hilariously funny account of the visit which the London teenager Minnie pays her family who have emigrated to Australia and the futile attempts she makes to Come Out to them, is another novel which extends the critique of heterosexuality to sex in general. Adopting an approach similar to Wittig's and Butler's, Livia concentrates attention on the ability of lesbianism to destabilize conventional models of sex, along with the heterosexist assumptions which they reflect. Laura's discovery that her sister Minnie may be lesbian has an unsettling effect on her, opening up chasms of unsuspected doubts and fears. As well as leading her to question her own sexual identity and her enjoyment of sex with men, it undermines the empirical 'common sense' view of sex and romance to which she previously subscribed:

> It had blown the gaff on the clear everyday world of true love and common sense. Now anyone could come at you from nowhere and accuse you, and however much you proved your pent up passion for penetration, it was possible to answer 'yes' to their question [Are you a lesbian?]. You might not 'really' enjoy fucking, you might be faking, you might fancy your best friend. If you cut off from females and expressed admiration only for things male, you could be a latent homosexual living in bitter denial of your own nature.[17]

The humour of this passage, accentuated by the emphatic use of alliteration, stems not only from Laura's naive perspective but also from the contrast between the unproblematic view of sexual attraction as predictable and stable, which she previously held, and the view of it as something shifting and uncontrollable, which is unexpectedly thrust upon her.

Another motif employed in *Ruby Fruit Jungle* which is developed in the fiction of the 1980s, is the critique of conventions of romantic love and the sexual inequalities which they reflect and perpetuate. Russ treats these themes with a passion and urgency which are altogether new. The savagely ironic denunciation of the injustices of the male-dominated social system which Esther voices in *On Strike Against God* makes the breezy protests uttered by Brown's Molly sound decidedly lightweight. Esther's objections to the myth of romantic love are personal and deeply felt. She perceives that, by making women emotionally dependent on men, it separates them from their female peers. As she sardonically comments, after attending a faculty party where she is accused by a colleague's wife of being 'an emotional cripple' for failing to marry and bear children:

> I wouldn't mind living in a private world and only seeing my women friends, but all my women friends live in the middle of a kind of endless soap opera: does he love me, does he like me, why did he say that, what did he mean, he didn't call me, I want a permanent relationship but he says we shouldn't commit ourselves, his feelings are changing towards me, ought I to sleep with him, what did he mean by that, sex is getting worse, sex is getting better . . . I don't think I'm satisfying his needs, he says he has to work – crisis after crisis and none of it leading anywhere . . . I cannot get into this swamp or I will never get out: and if I start crying again I'll remember that I have no one to love, and if anyone treats me like that again, *I'll kill him* . . . (Russ 1987: 33, italics added)

The breathless and hysterical-sounding accumulation of clauses which comprise this passage, while making the reader smile, creates a devastating exercise in parody. It cleverly mimics the obsessive investment which many women place in romantic love, as well as the masochistic attitude it reflects. The anger and potential violence which, as is indicated by the concluding threat, 'I'll kill him', often underlie their protestations of devotion is a key theme in Russ's novel. Esther's fantasy of killing a man, which recurs at intervals throughout the text, looks forward to films such as Marlene Gorris's *A Question of Silence* (1984) and Ridley Scott's *Thelma and Louise* (1991), in which fantasy disturbingly becomes fact. It also provides the climax to the episode of 'Shredded Napkin' in which Esther, sitting alone in a café, is waylaid and verbally assaulted by a male colleague. He foists his company upon her, orders drinks – and proceeds to subject her to a barrage of thinly veiled insults. In constructing the dialogue between the two characters, Russ makes effective use of the device of 'the double text', employing it to emphasize the contradiction between Esther's external poise and her inner feelings of rage.

> 'I often wonder why women have careers,' said Shredded Napkin suddenly, showing his teeth. I don't think he can possibly be saying what I think he's saying. He isn't, of course. Never mind. I'll stand this

because Reality is dishing it out and I suppose I ought to learn to adjust to it. Besides, he may be sincere . . .

'Oh goodness, I don't know, the same thing that makes a man decide, I suppose,' I said, trying to look bland and disarming. 'Cheers.'

'Cheers,' he said. The drinks had come. He opened his mouth to say something and then appeared to relent; he traced circles with his forefinger on the table. Then he said, leaning forward:

'You're strange animals, you women intellectuals. Tell me: what's it like to be a woman?'

I took my rifle from behind my chair and shot him dead. 'It's like that,' I said. No, of course I didn't . . . It's not worth it, hating, and I am going to be mature and realistic and not care, not care. Not any more. (Russ 1987: 6)

This passage, as well as illustrating Russ's ability to juxtapose different dimensions of existence by allowing her protagonist's violent fantasy momentarily to shatter the decorous veneer of social life, also exemplifies her expertise in creating scenarios informed by black humour. She forges for herself a style which, in interweaving the contrary impulses of humour and anger, teeters precariously and disconcertingly between the two.

On Strike Against God, while exposing the humiliating treatment to which women academics are subjected and giving a critique of romantic love, also offers a critical commentary on the genre of the romance itself. In portraying Esther becoming disillusioned with men and forming a relationship with her colleague Jean, Russ parodically inverts the conventions of the heterosexual romance, in which the heroine exchanges the female friendships of her childhood for an involvement with a man. She also inverts its values and ideological perspectives. Whereas in the heterosexual romance female maturity is identified with the heroine falling in love with a man and becoming a wife and mother, in Russ's novel and others in which the protagonist has a similar trajectory,[18] it takes the form of her seeing through the myth of romantic love, rejecting relationships with men and centering her affections on a woman.

On Strike Against God is, of course, not the only example of lesbian comic fiction which parodies romance conventions. Anne Leaton's *Good Friends, Just* (1983) creates a more intricate and detailed exercise in parody. The latter brings together and interweaves two romance narratives, the one lesbian in content and the other heterosexual. In the lesbian narrative the protagonist Maddy, who is spending a holiday in Turkey with her bisexual friend Georgina with whom she is in love, flirts with her and tries to persuade her to have an affair. She also attempts, with Georgina's assistance, to save their Turkish friend Melek from being coerced into an arranged marriage. In the heterosexual narrative Maddy and Georgina inadvertently become entangled with the two Turkish men Haluk Bey and his friend

Hasan who, unaware of the women's sexual orientation, try to seduce them. Humour arises from the clash and interaction which occurs between these two contrary storylines. The lesbian narrative frequently intercepts the heterosexual one, undermining its seriousness and making its events appear comic. Maddy, who acts as the link between the two, finds herself the unwilling object of Hasan's amorous attentions. He addresses her as 'sweetling'[19] and pays her pretty compliments. An amusing incongruity occurs between the roles of sex object and silent doll which he assigns to her, and the independent, articulate personality which the reader knows she has. Complex reversals of power also take place between the two characters. Hasan thinks that he is dominating and controlling her but, in actual fact, Maddy sees through his seduction game and cleverly manipulates him.

Lesbian existence

Accompanying the critique of heterosexuality which, as is illustrated in the previous section, occupies a prominent place in lesbian comic fiction, is the multifaceted topic of lesbian existence. This encompasses themes such as Coming Out, personal relationships, and the complexities of the lesbian social scene. It also comprises socio-political aspects of lesbian life, including the attitude of the general public towards homosexuality and items of government legislation which affect, directly or indirectly, the situation of lesbians and gay men.

Coming Out is a theme of major importance in the politically oriented fiction of the 1970s and early 1980s. Works such as Riley's *All That False Instruction* and Toder's *Choices*, which represent lesbian feminism as a challenge to patriarchal power and social structures, treat it in a positive and heroic light. While admitting that the individual's disclosure of her lesbian orientation may initially result in persecution and ostracization, they depict it as winning her, in the long run, the rewards of independence, self-respect and a place in the lesbian community. Lesbian comic novels such as Livia's *Relatively Norma* and Russ's *On Strike Against God* question these optimistic assumptions by concentrating attention on the indignities and pitfalls of Coming Out.

The attempts which Minnie makes to Come Out to her family Down Under in Livia's *Relatively Norma* are represented as the reverse of heroic. They strike the reader as ludicrous and absurd. Her various relatives are either too engrossed in their own activities to be interested in her sexual orientation or are too embarrassed by the topic of lesbianism to want to know about it. Minnie's sister, in her usual pragmatic fashion, queries the wisdom of Coming Out. Pinpointing the contradiction of confessing to be lesbian in a society which is rampantly homophobic, she asks the common-sense question, 'Who would voluntarily tell someone they were a pervert?'

(p. 37) In the context of this remark, Minnie's repeated attempts to Come Out appear doomed to deflation and failure – as, in fact, they are. In a series of amusing episodes set in such incongruous locations as a trampolining session and a Sunday morning traffic jam, she strives to inform her relatives of her lesbianism. However, she chooses her moment's badly – with the result that they either disbelieve her, are uninterested in her confession or fail to hear it. The novel's critique is directed not at the act of Coming Out per se but at the obsessive and egocentric preoccupation with the topic which some lesbians display. It also humorously exposes the excuses which heterosexuals employ to avoid confronting and discussing the subject of lesbianism.

As well as undermining the positive aspects of Coming Out, *Relatively Norma* also questions the significance of lesbianism (or any form of sexual identification) as the key to personal identity. A dominant theme in the novel, reflected in the fact that the protagonist assumes the alternative names of Minnie and Milly, is multiple selves and identities. We are told in the opening chapter that:

> After years of searching Minnie had given up on the 'real her' and called this other 'Milly'. They could have been made for each other. Milly was adept at being whoever anyone else wanted her to be. Minnie would draw people out and get them talking about themselves, their jobs, their preferences, and Milly would obligingly correspond with their vision of the world. (Livia 1982: 9)

Since, as this passage illustrates, the individual has more than one identity, there can scarcely be a single definitive key to it.

Works of lesbian comic fiction published in the 1980s and 1990s, as well as exploring the theme of Coming Out, also introduce episodes poking fun at the lesbian social scene and its conventions. The increasing willingness of lesbians to laugh at themselves is, as critics point out,[20] a healthy sign, indicating a new found sense of confidence. Episodes in *Relatively Norma* illustrate this. Livia comments satirically on the propensity of lesbians to fire 'direct, hostile questions' (Livia 1982: 26) at one another and ridicules their hypocritical approach to dress. When Minnie, newly arrived in Australia, is invited to a party, her feelings of pleasurable anticipation are undermined by worries about what she should wear. As Livia ironically comments, 'She would turn up not knowing if dresses had hit the Perth feminist scene yet. Of course, clothes didn't matter at all, except that they did enormously, especially when everybody would be seeing her for the first time and judging her accordingly' (p. 36).

Other writers besides Livia also explore the absurdities of lesbian social life. Namjoshi in *The Conversations of Cow*, a text which interweaves radical feminist perspectives with motifs from Indian mythology, examines the lesbian tendency to engage in role-play and imitate heterosexual codes of behaviour. Suniti, happily involved in a relationship with Bhadravati, makes the mistake, in her desire for 'pattern'[21] and order, of suggesting that they formalize the relationship. When told that marriage is out of the question, she changes her request to 'Ought we not to settle down?' (Namjoshi 1985: 89) Before she has time to repent the idea, she finds herself trapped in a parodic version of heterosexual role-play. Bhadravati, who is in fact a goddess, has taken her at her word and transformed the two of them into a conventional heterosexual couple. Assuming the identity of the chauvinistic Bud, she treats Suniti patronizingly — and insists, against her will, on carrying her suitcase and fussing over her. Meanwhile, poor Suniti is reduced to the role of 'robot companion' (p. 106).

The incidents of prejudice and discrimination frequently experienced by lesbians in everyday life is another topic which receives analysis in the lesbian comic novel. For Livia to choose as the target of her satire examples of bigotry and lesbian baiting, as she does in *Relatively Norma*, strikes one initially as inappropriate and odd. Topics of this depressing kind would seem unlikely to appeal to the reader who is looking for a laugh and a light read. In one episode Minnie, spending Christmas with her family and 'lulled into a false sense of security by a full stomach and a wine fumed brain' (Livia 1982: 21), finds herself in the embarrassing position of having to sit through a television showing of a film with a lesbophobic slant (an adaptation of D.H. Lawrence's 'The Fox') and endure her sister's bigoted comments. In another, she and a girl friend attend a clinic at the local hospital. While sitting in the waiting room, they attract the attention of a group of yobs who, noticing their unfeminine image, take pleasure in baiting them (pp. 89–90). The function which these two episodes perform in the novel is clarified by the perspective which Livia adopts in treating them. In both, ridicule is directed not at the lesbian protagonist, with whom the reader is positioned to identify, but at the ignorant, stupid behaviour of the bigots and lesbian-baiters. In the incident of the television film Minnie's sister's homophobic comments are motivated, we discover, by feelings of personal insecurity; she is anxious to convince her boyfriend that her attitudes and responses are 'normal'. In the scene at the hospital the yobs emerge as considerably less intelligent than the two women whom they taunt. When one of them calls her a transvestite, Minnie, tickled by the inappropriateness of the term and its connotations of *The Rocky Horror Show*, collapses in a fit of giggles. The roles of aggressor and victim are thus temporarily reversed, and the yobs become the target of both Minnie's and the reader's humour. Although the episodes commence on a threatening note, their effect, on account of Livia's buoyantly comic viewpoint and style, is ultimately reassuring. By portraying her lesbian protagonist surviving certain commonplace incidents of prejudice and holding her own with a group of queer-baiters, she exorcises to a degree the threat which they pose. She renders them, if not harmless, at any rate manageable.

A theme which has recently come to the fore in British lesbian fiction is the politically topical one of the homophobic backlash, at present taking place in the United Kingdom, and the notorious Section 28, which both exemplifies it and gives it legal sanction.[22] Ellen Galford's *Queendom Come* utilizes the strategy of humour to expose the Section's oppressive effects and alert the reader's attention to the injustices perpetrated by the Tory government which, led by Margaret Thatcher, was responsible for instituting it.

Queendom Come playfully combines versions of Celtic myth with references to present-day lesbian life in Edinburgh. The ancient British Queen Albanna, appalled by the rise in unemployment and the destruction which Prime Minister Thatcher and her gang of 'pin-striped desperadoes'[23] are wreaking on Local Government and the Health Service, unexpectedly returns from the grave to succour the Scottish people in their hour of need. Satire is directed at the right-wing attitudes of the Government, ironically termed 'the Blue Reich' (Galford 1990: 11), and at Thatcher's pretensions to achieve absolute power. Queen Albanna finds her self-imposed mission to rid the country of the forces of tyranny by no means easy to achieve since, as she remarks to her high priestess, she is uncertain which particular 'queen' she should eliminate – 'the one who wears the crowns and costumes [Queen Elizabeth] or the other one [Thatcher] who bosses everyone about' (p. 109).

Wittily renaming Section 28 'Section 82 of the Sexual Normality Act', Galford illustrates its oppressive effects and the anxieties which it arouses. However, it is not only heterosexual society which is the target of her attack. She also criticizes the small minority of lesbians and gay men who, instead of joining their fellows in demonstrating against the Section, choose to collude with their oppressors by exploiting for mercenary motives the fears of the gay community. Combining a critique of the pressures imposed on lesbians and gay men to pass as straight with a dig at the current commercial vogue for 'lifestyle' products, she caustically describes how:

> One perspicacious entrepreneur sets up an agency called Designer Closets. For a handsome fee, he will provide clients [scared of losing their jobs on the grounds that they are gay] with the resources they need to protect their livelihoods: a customised heterosexual curriculum vitae, complete with photographs of loving spouse and bouncing babies, plus a complimentary gold wedding band. (p. 54)

As well as illustrating the injustices of the Section in the events which she recounts, Galford also weaves allusions to them into the fabric of the novel. Parodying the censorship of gay culture which it seeks to impose, she announces in an authorial aside that she has decided to erase a lesbian love scene since to represent a sexual encounter between women might have the effect of promoting homosexuality – and thus contravene the law.

Humorously exploiting 'a carnivalesque paradox',[24] she advises the reader to lay the book aside for fear of being corrupted:

> What happens next, I am not at liberty to disclose. Especially not under Section 82 of the new Sexual Normality Act. So, for your own protection, do not imagine waterfalls, nightingales, shooting stars, damask roses, or eagles on the wing; ignore all opening buttons, warm skin, moving hands, tongues, lips, fingers . . . Do not believe that anyone was pleased, fulfilled, ecstatic, or otherwise made happy . . . Otherwise you run the risk of being recruited, corrupted, polluted, and probably arrested. Take my advice and shut your ears and eyes. Or, better still, close this book, find a socially acceptable spouse of the opposite gender, turn off the lights and assume the missionary position . . . (p. 69)

A worrying feature of the Section, as the above passage implies, is its veiled attempt to discourage both the production and the enjoyment of lesbian and gay culture. *Queendom Come* illustrates that strategies of humour and parody, as well as being entertaining, furnish a vigorous means of protest.

Freaks and monsters

A stereotype and mythic image which is frequently projected onto the figure of the lesbian in patriarchal culture is that of *monster*. Society, as Pamella Farley observes, defines 'the normal' and 'the natural' in opposition to the image of 'the abnormal' and 'the unnatural' – and sees homosexuality and lesbianism as representing the latter: 'By definition heterosexuality denies homosexuality; but it both requires and suppresses the scapegoat. Her function is to be the unthinkable alternative.'[25]

In this oppressive system of binary opposites, Farley points out, homosexuality performs the negative function of being 'wrong, so heterosexuality can be right . . . bad, so it can be good . . . and unnatural, so it can be natural' (p. 270). The portrayal of the lesbian as signifying everything that is evil and unnatural, far from being a relic of a barbaric past, is a frequent feature of contemporary literature and film. It finds expression not only in popular fiction but also in 'literary' texts by women who enjoy a reputation as feminist. *The Bad Sister* (1978) by the British Emma Tennant furnishes a pertinent example. Meg, the witch-like leader of the radical feminist commune around which the narrative revolves, inveigles the heroine Ishbel into joining the group, seducing her with a vampirish kiss which punctures her skin and produces 'two scarlet lozenges'[26] of blood. Meg is identified throughout the text with black magic and the occult. She materializes to Ishbel displaying the monstrous appurtenances of 'a vast head' with 'snake locks' and a set of 'teeth as long and white and pointed as stalactites' (pp. 85–6).

Lesbian writers respond in various ways to the homophobic tradition of 'the lesbian as monster'. They employ a number of different strategies to challenge and revise it. Jewelle Gomez and Jody Scott appropriate and rework the image of the vampire. They treat it from a sympathetic viewpoint, utilizing it to explore the roles of deviant and outsider traditionally assigned to the lesbian. Bertha Harris, in a critical essay, employs the strategy of ironic inversion. Instead of rejecting the image of monster outright, as the reader expects, she ironically endorses and celebrates it. The lesbian represents, in Harris's view, an alternative image of womanhood to the passive, docile one constructed by patriarchy; she epitomises 'the Female enraged' and, as a result, manifests attributes which society regards as 'unspeakable'.[27]

Fictional texts which re-evaluate and subvert the image of the lesbian as a monster, it is interesting to note, are often transgressive in more than one respect. They interrogate and revise certain other stereotypes of femininity which society typecasts as repellent and 'monstrous'. These include the female alcoholic and the woman who is menopausal. They also focus on topics which contemporary Western culture regards as distasteful and unmentionable, such as mental disturbance, sexual relations between the elderly, and matters relating to death. That these disparate themes and motifs should appear together in a number of lesbian fictional texts is understandable, since they have more in common than one might initially suppose. They are all examples of the category which Kristeva defines as 'the abject'. She denotes by this term phenomena and events which society or the individual sees, on a psychological or a material plane, as unclean and tainting and thus seeks to eject. However, even when they are expelled, they continue to haunt us and refuse to disappear.[28]

Arnold's *Sister Gin* published at the early date of 1975, is centrally concerned with 'the abject' and society's attempts to expel it. The novel makes inventive use of the theme of the divided self and creates an original interplay between realism and fantasy. It utilizes humour, frequently the disconcerting kind, to give an insight into the despised position of the lesbian in American culture and to challenge derogatory attitudes towards the elderly.

In portraying her protagonist Su and recounting her 'monstrous' story, Arnold, like Harris, employs a strategy of inversion. Instead of rejecting the image of the lesbian as monster, she ironically endorses it, giving it new and subversive significance. Su's trajectory is, in social terms, a very depressing one. She deteriorates in the course of the novel from being a model of female intelligence and poise, with a prestigious, well-paid job as a book-reviewer, to the role of angry, unemployed alcoholic. This disturbing metamorphosis occurs as a result of her acting on the promptings of her rebellious alter ego Sister Gin who, becoming increasingly irrepressible and domineering as the narrative progresses, forces her to flout convention by Coming Out to her employers and demanding that they publish reviews of lesbian books. By the end of the novel Su has become the prototype of 'the Female enraged'; she displays attributes which, judged by conventional standards of femininity, are 'unspeakable'. Her unpredictable behaviour and sudden outbursts of rage make even her friends mistrust her and shun her company. This transformation, the novel indicates, rather than reflecting her personal inadequacies, functions as an indictment of the repressive nature of American society which, by treating the lesbian as a pariah, drives her to become a self-destructive fury.

Su's monstrous metamorphosis, though losing her friends and placing her, from a social point of view, beyond the pale, brings with it compensations. One of these is a new, enlightened perspective on the ageing process and old age itself. The novel opens with her experiencing the worst effects of the menopause. Hot flushes, loss of memory and an inability to concentrate are some of the symptoms which she manifests. As she admits, she feels as if she has been transformed into a hideous caricature of old age: 'I'm just what everyone always says old women are like . . . a forgetful, distracted, silly old biddy . . .'[29] A significant irony in this perceptive and deviously witty novel is that it is the 77-year-old Mamie Carter, with whom Su has a brief love affair, who is portrayed as achieving the feat of reconciling her to the facts of ageing.

Mamie Carter functions as a vehicle for Arnold to deconstruct the pejorative stereotype of old age, accepted by contemporary Western culture, and replace it with a positive one. The popularly held view of elderly women as physically frail and politically conservative is challenged by Mamie's successful organization of a feminist activist group. The notion that they are unattractive and uninterested in sex is refuted by the passion which she inspires in Su – and by the vitality of her own erotic response. Rejecting the prejudiced assumption that sexual activity in old age is out of place and disgusting, the novel concentrates attention on its pleasures. Su finds Mamie's ageing body attractive. She tenderly savours 'the sight of her dimpled flesh, infinite dimples winking in their softness, skin so old it had lost all abrasives, rid itself of everything that can shield the body against the world . . .' (Arnold 1979: 128). She lovingly contemplates Mamie's 'sparse [pubic] hair curling like steel – there was strength between her legs and no dough there where the flesh was fluid enough to slip away from the bone and leave that tensed grain hard as granite and her upright violent part like an animal nose against Su's palm' (pp. 129–30). Commenting on her enjoyment of sex, she humorously remarks, 'I just never imagined that the delights of old age would include the fact of endlessly drawnout orgasms' (p. 129)!

Arnold's transgressive celebration of the pleasures of old age culminates in the representation of it as the most rewarding period of life, and in a description of the creative powers which it confers on the individual. Mamie Carter sagely affirms that 'Only in old age can one brain be all ages . . . Because the life of the mind is more intense . . . and because the novelist creates by rounding out, filling in, and rearranging everyday, the old mind is the complete novelist.' Inverting the stereotype of the genius who is forever young, she insists that 'It's not necessary to be old to think old. It has been said that geniuses are forever old' (p. 189). The novel ends on an optimistic note with Su ceasing to worry about the ageing process. On the contrary, she finds herself regretting the fact that, in Mamie Carter's eyes, she is 'just not old enough' (p. 195).

Works of lesbian comic fiction published in the 1980s and 1990s, though seldom achieving the radical vision of Arnold's *Sister Gin*, continue to challenge homophobia and interrogate and revise the image of the lesbian as monster. An aim of Livia's *Relatively Norma*, as the title signals, is to problematize the concept of 'the normal' by encouraging the reader to perceive just how relative and artificial it is. A key episode in the novel is the discovery, unwillingly made by Minnie's sister, that standards of normality are by no means absolute: 'Laura had to accept the awful truth. Heterosexuality wasn't normal, there wasn't any normal for it to be' (Livia 1982: 55).

Relatively Norma employs a number of different strategies to question and subvert patriarchal concepts of normality. It inverts the image of monster by assigning it not to the lesbian protagonist Minnie but to the characters who identify as heterosexual. Minnie's lesbianism strikes us as a mere minor eccentricity in comparison with the aberrant and bizarre behaviour of her various relatives. Her father, a psychiatrist by profession, is a sadist who denies her mother housekeeping money and refuses to allow her medication for her asthma attacks on the grounds that he regards them as psychosomatic. Her mother is a reformed alcoholic who, suddenly wearying of the maternal role, formally dissolves the bond with her children and vanishes from their lives (pp. 174–80). Her sister Ingrid suffers from bulimia. The characters who emerge as the least aberrant and odd are, in fact, certainly elderly female figures. Here again Livia employs the device of inversion. She represents these characters not as weak and marginal, as is generally the case in contemporary Western literature, but as intelligent and powerful. In a comic episode which introduces elements of the surreal, a group of elderly women are depicted entrapping the members of the Police, who are harassing them, in a web of knitting wool (pp. 187–8). The novel, like *Sister Gin*, also refers to the taboo topic of sexual relations between the elderly and introduces a love scene between two elderly women (p. 161).

Another topic which *Relatively Norma* explores is the psychology of prejudice. It investigates the motives which prompt people to cling to concepts of 'the normal' and 'the natural' and to stigmatize others as 'abnormal' and 'perverse'. Minnie's sister Laura has spent much of her childhood in an orphanage. She clings desperately to standards of normal behaviour in order to compensate for her unconventional and deprived upbringing.

In exploring the psychology of prejudice, Livia adopts a humorously cynical approach. She illustrates that incidents of prejudice and bigotry, far from being unusual, are an integral part of human behaviour, reflecting the power struggles in which we all engage. The exchange of insults which takes place between the characters is, in certain episodes, fast and furious. It assumes at times the appearance of a ritualized game, resembling the cursing-matches, ridicule and verbal abuse[30] which Bakhtin describes as a feature of carnivalesque mirth. Minnie, on hearing herself ridiculed as 'a bloody pervert' and 'an insult to the human race', retaliates by mentally deriding the youths who are baiting her as 'fuckwits' and 'dick-heads' (Livia 1982: 86–8). The humorous absurdity of the language of prejudice is acknowledged, as is illustrated by the reference to the label 'pinko commie queer' (p. 73). The novel also recognizes the fact that lesbians, ridiculed by society as 'lepers' and 'perverts', are not the only people to suffer verbal abuse. Elderly female figures are dismissively described as 'old bats' (p. 32); Minnie's sister Ingrid is mocked because of her German-sounding name; and Johnny, the manager of the hairdressing salon where she works, is ridiculed on account of his homosexuality. 'He's not a bloke, he's a poofta', one of his employees contemptuously remarks (p. 34).

By highlighting the arbitrary and commonplace nature of prejudice and transposing exchanges of insults to the transgressive plane of the carnivalesque, Livia emphasizes their comic aspect. While confronting their existence, she temporarily averts the threat which they pose.

Certain of the strategies employed in *Sister Gin* and *Relatively Norma* are developed by Winterson in *Oranges Are Not the Only Fruit*. In the latter, conventional standards of normality are again deconstructed and shown to be relative and artificial. When Jeanette is in primary school she is puzzled by the fact that the teacher criticizes the gloomy but original design of the sampler which she has made, while praising the tritely pretty piece of work produced by one of her class-mates. The incident leads her to perceive that:

> What constitutes a problem is not the thing, or the environment where we find the thing, but the conjunction of the two; something unexpected in a usual place (our favourite aunt in our favourite poker parlour) or something usual in an unexpected place (our favourite poker in our favourite aunt) . . .[31]

This observation acquires additional significance, moving from a comic dimension to a serious one, in the light of subsequent events – namely Jeanette's discovery of her lesbianism and the relationship which she forms with Melanie. Sexual passions which appear perfectly natural to the two girls are regarded by Pastor Finch, in the context of his puritanical religious beliefs, as decidedly *un*natural.

Oranges Are Not the Only Fruit also inverts the image of monster, by assigning it not to the lesbian characters but to representatives of patriarchal masculinity. Young Jeanette, on overhearing a neighbour remark that she has married a pig, takes the comment literally. She believes that the husband really is a pig. 'It was hard to tell he was a pig. He was clever, but his eyes were close together and his skin bright pink. I tried to imagine him without his clothes on. Horrid' (p. 71). This reference to the animal world is fancifully elaborated. It shifts, in postmodernist manner, from being an image for the repulsive aspects of male physical appearance to one representing 'men as beasts'. This, in turn, becomes a vehicle for describing male duplicity and cunning: 'And beasts are crafty, they disguise themselves like you and I. Like the wolf in "Little Red Riding Hood" . . . Did that mean that all over the globe, in all innocence, women were marrying beasts?' (pp. 72–3)

A motif with connotations of the monstrous which plays a central role in *Oranges Are Not the Only Fruit* is the demon. The Pastor, when accusing Jeanette and Melanie of demonic possession, employs it in a conventional manner as a signifier of supernatural evil. However, it is subsequently transformed into a signifier of individualism and personal freedom when the Orange Demon unexpectedly materializes to Jeanette and engages her in conversation. Hopping onto the mantelpiece, he cheerfully tells her that everyone has a demon and that if she insists on keeping hers, she will have 'a difficult, different time' (p. 109).

Winterson is not, of course, the first writer to identify demons with liberation and to portray her/his protagonist conversing with them. In *The Marriage of Heaven and Hell* (1790) by William Blake, a poet to whom Winterson alludes,[32] angels are associated with oppression while the denizens of Hell represent liberation. A devil, appearing to the poet in a flame, reinterprets the Scriptures from a radical viewpoint and gives him moral counsel.

Esther, the protagonist of Russ's *On Strike Against God*, also has her own personal demon (daemon). He represents the rebellious facet of her psyche and, in keeping with this, encourages her to stand up for herself when her sexist colleagues ridicule her. He also prompts her to flout convention by embarking on a relationship with her friend Jean. Though initially resenting his intrusion on her life, Esther eventually decides that she likes him. She admits that, with his 'conscientious clawlets out, a-lert and a-ware', he is 'woman's best friend' (Russ 1987: 30). The Orange Demon in Winterson's novel carries similar associations of sexual liberation. Like the demon in Blake's work he is a source of radical wisdom and, like Russ's, he encourages the narrator to withstand the bigoted attitudes of the local community and remain true to her own desires.

Oranges Are Not the Only Fruit, as well as reworking from a lesbian feminist perspective images of the monstrous, also shares with *Sister Gin* and *Relatively Norma* a focus on topics which contemporary Western culture regards as either insignificant or socially taboo. Middle-aged and elderly women play a major part in the narrative, the physical facts of death are confronted and, in the episode in which Jeanette gives Melanie the flowers which she has taken from the cemetery, the connections between love and death are acknowledged.

The novel has been rightly acclaimed for its originality and inventiveness. However, it also merits praise for continuing a tradition of lesbian comic fiction which is notable for its diversity and flexibility. This tradition, having developed in the 1970s and 1980s, continues to respond to new circumstances, social and intellectual, and to entertain and empower readers with its interplay of humour and political radicalism.

Notes

1 See Zimmerman, 'Lesbians Like This and That', ed. cit., p. 4.
2 Rich, 'Compulsory Heterosexuality and Lesbian Existence', ed. cit., pp. 26–51.
3 Wittig, 'One Is Not Born a Woman', in *The Straight Mind and Other Essays* (1992), pp. 11–20.
4 Butler, 'Imitation and Gender Insubordination', ed. cit., p. 23.
5 Little, *Comedy and the Woman Writer: Woolf, Spark and Feminism* (University of Nebraska Press, 1983), p. 6.
6 See Hilary Hinds, '*Oranges Are Not the Only Fruit*: Reaching Audiences Other Lesbian Texts Cannot Reach', in *New Lesbian Criticism*, ed. cit., pp. 153–72.
7 Case discusses Split Britches Cabaret in 'Toward a Butch-Femme Aesthetic', ed. cit., pp. 288–96.
8 See Smyth, *Lesbians Talk Queer Notions*, ed. cit., pp. 11–27.
9 See Chapter 1, note 17.
10 Cixous, 'The Laugh of the Medusa', in *New French Feminisms*, ed. cit., p. 255.
11 Kristeva, *Revolution in Poetic Language*, translated by Margaret Waller (Columbia University Press, 1984), pp. 224–5. Bakhtin also discusses the liberating effect of laughter in *Problems of Dostoevsky's Poetics*, ed. cit., pp. 126–7, 165.
12 Russ, *On Strike Against God* (Women's Press, 1987), p. 8. Subsequent references are to this edition and in the text.
13 Bakhtin, *Rabelais and His World*, translated by Helene Iswolsky (MIT Press, 1968), pp. 11, 34.
14 Nancy A. Walker discusses the woman humorist's role in *A Very Serious Thing: Women's Humour and American Culture* (University of Minnesota Press, 1988), pp. 9–37.
15 Boucher, 'Lesbian Artists', ed. cit., p. 43.
16 Brown, *Ruby Fruit Jungle* (Corgi, 1978), p. 80. Subsequent references are to this edition and in the text.

17 Livia, *Relatively Norma* (Onlywomen, 1982), p. 51. Subsequent references are to this edition and in the text.

18 See Anne Leaton, *Good Friends, Just* (Chatto and Windus, 1983). For references to critical studies of the romance, see Chapter 4, note 14.

19 Leaton, *Good Friends, Just*, ed. cit., p. 68.

20 See Susan J. Wolfe, 'Ingroup Lesbian Feminist Political Humor', paper given at the Midwest Modern Language Association, Minneapolis, November 1980, pp. 1–2. Quoted in Walker, *A Very Serious Thing*, ed. cit., p. 163.

21 Namjoshi, *The Conversations of Cow* (Onlywomen, 1985), p. 89. Subsequent references are to this edition and in the text.

22 See Chapter 1, note 17.

23 Galford, *Queendom Come* (Virago, 1990), p. 71. Subsequent references are to this edition and in the text.

24 John Lechte explains that, according to Kristeva, 'A carnivalization might occur when the libertine novel itself "seriously" included a proposal for its being censored within its own discourse' (*Julia Kristeva*, Routledge, 1990, p. 108).

25 Farley, 'Lesbianism and the Social Function of Taboo', in Hester Eisenstein and Alice Jardine (eds) *The Future of Difference* (G.K. Hall, 1980), p. 270.

26 Tennant, *The Bad Sister* (Picador, 1979), p. 87.

27 Harris, 'What We Mean to Say: Notes toward Defining the Nature of Lesbian Literature', *Heresies*, 3 (1977), p. 7.

28 Lechte, *Julia Kristeva*, ed. cit., pp. 158–62.

29 Arnold, *Sister Gin* (Women's Press, 1979), p. 43. Subsequent references are to this edition and in the text.

30 Bakhtin, *Problems of Dostoevsky's Poetics*, ed. cit., pp. 125, 130.

31 Winterson, *Oranges Are Not the Only Fruit* (Pandora, 1985), p. 45.

32 Winterson, *Oranges Are Not the Only Fruit*, ed. cit., p. 108.

6

New developments in fiction: fantasy and sex

To someone who asked her what is the most mysterious thing in the world, Phenarete invariably responded, 'I don't know anything in the world more mysterious than desire in its manifestations, its appearances, its disappearances.'

(Monique Wittig and Sande Zeig 1980: 42)

New departures

Some of the developments which have recently taken place in lesbian fiction have already been discussed in this study. One of the most striking is the work which is taking place in the field of genre fiction, as writers increasingly recognize that forms appropriated from the dominant culture make apt and versatile vehicles for treating lesbian themes. Experimentation with genre is linked, as we have seen, to the rejection of the direct methods of political protest employed in the 1970s and early 1980s and the utilization, instead, of strategies reflecting impulses of pleasure and play. It also indicates a new interest, practical as well as intellectual, in popular kinds of writing. The interaction and tension which occurs between certain mainstream genres and motifs (the thriller, the comic novel, the investigator, the monster) and the lesbian perspectives applied to them, generate challenging and innovative effects, as illustrated in the previous two chapters. Although in the work of some writers these remain on the level of entertainment, in that of others, such as O'Rourke, Wings, Galford and Winterson, they assume a political dimension. The revision of popular genres functions in many cases as an alternative form of protest and resistance to the overtly political methods adopted by writers in the 1970s.

The experimentation at present taking place in the field of genre highlights other facets of contemporary lesbian fiction too. The most obvious is its diversity. No longer is it valid to think in terms of 'the lesbian novel'. Instead, we need to think in terms of a variety of different genres and kinds.

That this diversity exists illustrates the commercial success which lesbian writing is currently enjoying. As publishers' lists and the shelves of book-shops illustrate, it is a flourishing literary category. Fiction is one of its most popular subsections.

The effect which the expansion and diversification of lesbian writing in the 1980s and 1990s has had on the quality of the texts produced is a matter of controversy. Some critics argue that, with the exception of a few brilliant works, the literary value of lesbian fiction is in decline. They complain that the forces of commercialism, combined with the emphasis on sex, which, as we shall see, is a feature of many present-day works, result in writing which is mechanical and cliché-ridden.[1] Novels introduce sex scenes which are unrelated to plot or character, while the positive images of lesbian social interaction and personal relationships which characterized the fiction pro-duced in the 1970s have been replaced by an emphasis on 'pain and divi-sion'.[2] Comments of this kind, though containing an element of truth, are in my opinion over-pessimistic. A problematic aspect of the current preoc-cupation with sex is that it encourages writers to concentrate exclusively on characters who are young, able-bodied and free from family commitments, while ignoring the themes of lesbian community, lesbian motherhood[3] and relations between older women which were popular in the 1970s. However, it simultaneously has the advantage of promoting a focus on role-play, sexual fantasy and the construction of lesbian sexuality, the ex-ploration of which is long overdue. Moreover, themes and perspectives which some readers disparage as cynical and depressing, others regard as a valid response to the changes which have occurred in theoretical ap-proaches to lesbianism and in the situation of lesbians and gay men. The novels of Winterson, Galford and Schulman, discussed in this chapter, deserve to be seen in the latter favourable light. They are intellectually adventurous and inventively rework traditional modes of writing such as fantasy, the fairy tale and the romance. They also successfully incorporate new developments in the field of theory and narrativity, ones associated with postmodernism in particular.[4]

Here it is necessary to point out that lesbian theorists and writers are by no means merely passive recipients of postmodernist ideas and strategies. On the contrary, they have made an important contribution to their growth and articulation. In the 1970s they were among the first to attempt to denaturalize phenomena and institutions such as heterosexuality, the family and patriarchal social structures and, by writing from the perspective of a marginalized minority group, to challenge the concepts of a 'master narrative' and a 'universalist' point of view. They are also at the fore in re-evaluating and reworking non-canonical forms of fiction, such as the thriller and the romance. In addition, writers of comic and satiric fiction utilize strategies of parody and inversion for purposes of political analysis and protest.

The works of fiction considered below develop these strategies and introduce others of a similar kind. By juxtaposing contrary discourses, value-systems and story-lines, they question the unitary representation of subjectivity and culture, and rupture the apparently seamless web of the realist text. Winterson and Galford, in treating episodes from history, bring to the foreground the viewpoint of marginalized figures such as women and the working-class. DeLynn and Schulman, influenced by Queer Politics and the writing of the lesbian sexual radicals, investigate different sexual identifications and examine the links between fantasy and sex. Like Wings, another writer whose work displays postmodern traits, they subvert the conventions of the romance by introducing elements of parody and pastiche. The novels and stories of these writers illustrate the continuing vitality of lesbian fiction, and its ability to respond creatively to new attitudes and themes.

Fantasy and narrativity

'Everyone who tells a story tells it differently just to remind us that everybody sees it differently', Winterson writes in *Oranges Are Not the Only Fruit*.[5] The quotation illustrates the interest in narrativity and in exploring connections between narrative and point of view which is a feature not only of this particular novel but also of the other works of fiction discussed in this section. While differing in subject matter and design, they display a similarly intricate structure and an interest in experimenting with genre and style.

Oranges Are Not the Only Fruit, an example of lesbian comic fiction, has links with certain other fictional forms. It is, in fact, an up-to-date version of the two genres which writers focusing on lesbian feminist themes in the 1970s most frequently employed – the *bildungsroman* and the Coming Out novel. Winterson's novel disproves the critical view that the latter genre is outmoded by introducing a number of motifs associated with it.[6] These include the naive but intelligent protagonist who feels cramped by the narrow confines of her provincial surroundings, her discovery of her lesbian orientation through a first love affair, her subsequent betrayal by her lover who reverts to heterosexuality, and the punitive treatment meted out to her by her family and the community. All these motifs occur in Riley's *All That False Instruction*, while some of them are also employed in other early works of lesbian fiction such as Brown's *Ruby Fruit Jungle*, Roberts's *A Piece of the Night* and Toder's *Choices*. The fact that, far from appearing out of date and old-fashioned, they continue to arouse interest and generate a spark of recognition in the reader is a salutary reminder of how little the basic facts of lesbian existence have changed in the United Kingdom in the past twenty years. As the calls which my co-workers and I receive on our local lesbian line illustrate, while the teenager in the process of discovering her lesbianism can, if she knows where to find the number, contact her local line for advice and support, and can, if she knows the right institution to which to apply, attend the occasional seminar in lesbian studies at college or university, she is none the less likely to experience similiar anxieties, feelings of confusion and parental disapproval to those encountered by her predecessors in the 1970s.[7] To the member of the line taking the call these emotions and events may be a thing of the past, but to the teenager making it they are of immediate significance and pressingly urgent.

Oranges Are Not the Only Fruit treats the motifs from the Coming Out novel mentioned above unconventionally, giving them new relevance. Like Livia's *Relatively Norma*, an earlier example of the genre which, as well as utilizing humour for political purposes, introduces anti-realist episodes and authorial digressions, it interweaves fantasy and realism, interspersing Jeanette's account of her youth in a Northern provincial town with a series of subsidiary narratives of a fabulous and fairy tale kind. Some commentators and critics mistakenly regard these as superfluous. The television adaptation of the novel omitted them, presumably in order to concentrate attention on Jeanette's social circumstances and, by adopting a realist emphasis, allow the viewer a greater degree of identification. Duncker, who criticizes the anti-realist episodes in *Relatively Norma* on the grounds that they make 'sudden fissures in the realist text',[8] similarly dismisses them as 'not necessary' (p. 179). The fantasy episodes in *Oranges*, however, far from being superfluous, are an integral part of the novel and perform a number of important functions. The interplay of narratives which they create highlights the part which fantasy plays in the construction of the adolescent psyche and gives a more complex and multifaceted representation of subjectivity than is usually found in the Coming Out novel. As Winterson herself comments, hinting at this, 'You can read *Oranges* in spirals . . . I don't really see the point of reading in straight lines. We don't think like that and we don't live like that. Our mental processes are closer to a maze than a motorway . . .'[9]

Oranges Are Not the Only Fruit, while rejecting a unitary model of subjectivity in favour of a delineation of fantasy identities and multiple selves, also, in true postmodernist spirit, envisages and depicts subjectivity itself in terms of narrativity. Jeanette, instead of uncovering a single, static identity, constructs for herself a series of shifting, fluid selves by means of the acts of storytelling and fabulation in which she engages. Storytelling enables her to acknowledge, in the words of Cixous, the existence of her 'monsters . . . jackals . . . fellow-creatures . . . fears'.[10]

In the tale of Sir Perceval Jeanette adopts the persona of an errant knight embarking on a spiritual quest. Emphasis is placed not on the heroic aspects of the chivalric tradition but on the disintegration of the company of the Round Table and the feelings of disillusion in which it results (Winterson

1985: 128, 134). In the story of Winnett, an idiosyncratic version of the
tale of the Sorcerer's Apprentice, she relives and re-evaluates her stormy
relationship with her mother (pp. 141–8). She transposes into a fairy tale
form the power-struggles and conflicts which it involves and the painful rift
in which it culminates. The representation of the bond between mother
and daughter in terms of the attachment between a sorcerer and his apprentice emphasizes its irrational aspect, acknowledging the 'magical' power
which it wields. The fact that a gender displacement occurs and the figure
of the mother is represented not by a witch but by a male wizard, universal-
izes the theme of power relations between parent and child and illustrates
Winterson's refusal to be tied to biologistic assumptions. In 'the theatres of
the mind'[11] gender differences are subverted and our desires, anxieties and
fears acted out by a myriad different figures, both male and female. As
Cixous, commenting on this, remarks, 'I is this matter, personal, exuberant,
lively, masculine, feminine, or other in which I delights me and distresses
me.'[12]

The displacement of the rift between Jeanette and her mother into the
realm of fairy tale is significant in other ways as well. As a student who
attended a seminar which I gave on the novel observed, it renders its pain
bearable and enables Jeanette to view it with a degree of emotional
detachment.

Winterson's imaginative treatment of fairy tale and fable, as well as being
a vehicle for representing Jeanette's shifting identities and the displacements
which fantasy enacts, also has literary and ideological import. From a literary point of view, the interplay of different narratives and genres which it
generates creates an exercise in intertextuality, illustrating the fact that all
texts are composed of grafts from earlier ones.[13] On an ideological level, it
functions as a strategy to question and challenge the patriarchal values
associated with the fairy tale. Images of femininity constructed by a male-
dominated culture are interrogated and problematized. In the tale of the
princess who was so sensitive that she wept for the death of a moth
(Winterson 1985: 9), the stereotypically feminine attributes of narcissism
and sentimentality are confronted and rejected, while the story of the
princes' search for a flawless woman examines male ideals of femininity and
exposes their oppressive effect on flesh-and-blood women (pp. 61–7). The
story of Red Riding Hood (p. 73) is transformed into a fable illustrating a
young girl's feelings of anxiety about heterosexual relations and male duplicity. As in other works of postmodern fiction by women, 'story telling is
not presented as a privatized form of experience' but becomes 'a political
and historical act'.[14]

The most important text the authority and ideology of which the novel
questions and undermines is, of course, the Old Testament, the master text
of Western civilization. A strategy which Winterson employs to achieve
this is to place biblical motifs in new and incongruous contexts. The titles of

the books of the Old Testament function as structuring devices in Jeanette's Coming Out story. Biblical episodes and themes also have their authority undercut by appearing in settings which are comically inappropriate. The text 'The summer is ended and we are not yet saved' features incongruously on a child's sampler (p. 39), while Elsie, in re-creating the episode of the Three Men in the Fiery Furnace, uses the unusual medium of *mice* (p. 31). Even bearing in mind the various weird and wonderful materials which postmodern artists employ, this must surely rank as a first. It surpasses in ingenuity the activities of Margaret Atwood's experimenter with post-modern art forms, the Royal Porcupine,[15] who uses the freeze-dried corpses of animals to construct his works. His exhibits, eye-catching though they certainly are, are dead, whereas the novelty of Elsie's depends on the fact that they are very much alive!

Winterson's skill in interplaying different intellectual and literary ap-proaches, illustrated by her reworking of motifs from the 1970s Coming Out novel in the light of contemporary concepts of narrativity and subjec-tivity, is also apparent in her treatment of lesbianism. The focus which the novel places on woman-identified involvements reflects lesbian feminist attitudes, but its emphasis on the sexual aspect of lesbianism has more in common with the perspectives of the lesbian sexual radicals. While the network of female relationships which comprise Jeanette's life recalls Rich's theory of lesbian continuum, these relationships are not idealized or de-scribed uncritically. Although in some episodes women are portrayed as loving, strong and loyal, in others they are depicted as weak or tyrannical, willing to oppress their sisters by colluding with the representatives of patriarchy. Jeanette's adoptive mother is portrayed in a particularly ambig-uous light. Her character displays a contradictory though convincing amal-gam of courage and bigotry, imagination and callousness. Winterson's critical exposé of the acts of bigotry carried out in the name of religion, though including examples of compulsory heterosexuality, extends beyond it. In the tradition of Blake, whose radical concept of morality influences the novel, it encompasses sexual repression in general.

The interest in subjectivity and narrativity which informs *Oranges Are Not the Only Fruit* is developed in Winterson's subsequently published novel *Sexing the Cherry* (1989). In the latter, however, it takes a more complex form, since the interplay of narratives revolves around not one consciousness but two – the Dog-Woman's and that of her adopted son, Jordan. An additional complication arises from the fact that identities and psychological attributes are envisaged as transcending the boundaries of time and space. Jordan and the Dog-Woman are seventeenth-century fig-ures, and each has a twentieth-century double or counterpart who displays analogous qualities and attitudes. Or, to put it more accurately, as emerges toward the end of Winterson's novel, the two seventeenth-century figures function as alter egos for the present-day ones. The psychological and

political affinities between the Dog-Woman and her present-day counterpart are described particularly vividly. While the former invests her energies
in challenging religious bigotry and exterminating puritans, the latter devotes her life to ecological issues and spends her time fighting multi-
national companies in an attempt to stem the tide of environmental pollu-
tion. Both women are ridiculed by the general public as 'monsters' – the
Dog-Woman on account of her exceptional size and strength, which are
regarded as unfeminine, and the present-day figure on account of her
radical views and commitment to a politics of direct action.

The relevance of these four characters, and the specular relationship
existing between them, to the theme of subjectivity, is elucidated by Jordan's remark, 'The inward life tells us that we are multiple not single, and
that our one existence is really countless existences holding hands like those
cut-out paper dolls, but unlike the dolls never coming to an end.'[16] Jordan
also clarifies the fluid and shifting interaction between subject and alter ego
which typifies the novel. Uncertain whether the dancer with whom he is
infatuated and whom he spends his youth seeking is real or imaginary, he
asks the pertinent question, 'Was I searching for a dancer whose name I did
not know or was I searching for the dancing part of myself?' (Winterson
1990: 40) The ambiguous relationship which some of the characters bear to
reality – are they 'real' or imaginary, we are prompted to ask? – highlights
one of the novel's key themes. As Winterson playfully reminds us, by
drawing attention to the fictionality of the text and the acts of representation which its construction involves, the question is ultimately meaning-
less since all the characters portrayed in it are fictions.

The relevance of *Sexing the Cherry* to the topic of lesbianism is open to
question. It is certainly more indirect than any of the other texts discussed
in this study. Lesbianism does not enjoy, on the whole, a privileged status
but is represented, in a manner resembling the approach adopted by the
lesbian sexual radicals and the supporters of Queer Politics, as one of a
variety of sexual identifications and positions. These include homosexuality, bisexuality, heterosexuality, sadomasochism and celibacy. On certain occasions, however, it does assume prominence. Some episodes either
refer to it directly or treat themes and motifs which play a central part in the
lesbian cultural tradition.

In Winterson's innovative version of the story of the Twelve Dancing
Princesses (pp. 47–60) lesbian and woman-identified relationships take on
political significance, denoting female courage and resistance to patriarchal
power. In rewriting the fairy tale, Winterson portrays the princesses as
liberating themselves, in some cases by violent means, from their husbands'
control. Instead of living happily ever after in marital bliss, as convention
dictates, they set up home together in a female community. The various
narratives assigned to them highlight the social and economic power which
men wield, and the brutal punishments which they inflict on women if

they dare to transgress the conventional role of object of exchange by forming sexual relationships with one another.

Other episodes in the novel develop the denaturalization of phallocentric images of femininity and the problematization of heterosexual relations, along with the re-evaluation of the image of woman as monster, which, as illustrated in the previous chapter, play a pivotal part in contemporary lesbian fiction. The Dog-Woman and her activities serve as a vehicle for all three themes.

The Dog-Woman, a virtual giantess, is portrayed as a magnificently empowering figure. Her literary antecedents include the Baron Munchausen, Cyrano de Bergerac and characters from Rabelais. Her immense size and strength enable her to perform a number of incredible feats. These include tossing an elephant in the air and picking up men by the scruff of the neck 'the way a terrier does a rat' (Winterson 1990: 88). Though recognizing that her height, flat nose and heavy eyebrows conflict with conventional concepts of beauty, she none the less prides herself on being 'built in proportion'. A writer with a phallocentric viewpoint would no doubt treat her as a target of ridicule but Winterson, writing in the tradition of the lesbian/feminist re-evaluation of the image of woman as monster, treats her in a celebratory manner. She focuses attention on her heroic qualities and describes her as representing the rebellious, transgressive aspect of femininity which patriarchy attempts to suppress (p. 127).

A key role which the Dog-Woman plays in the novel is to problematize and 'disrupt'[17] heterosexuality. Her one and only experience of sexual intercourse, a bizarre event in which her male partner, on account of her vast size, feels 'like a tadpole in a pot' and is reduced to 'burrowing down the way ferrets do' (pp. 106–7), cleverly avoids making her look ridiculous. On the contrary, it has the effect of defamiliarizing the sex act and making it and her partner appear absurd. It also parodies the misogynistic fantasy of the vagina dentata.

Another novel which revises traditional genres from a feminist perspective and brings together characters from different historical periods is Galford's *The Fires of Bride* (1986). It creates an original interplay of discourses, interweaving materials drawn from such varied and apparently incompatible sources as Scottish myth, Gothic romance and lesbian theory. By reworking Gothic images and motifs and employing them to treat lesbian themes, the novel challenges the representation of lesbianism as a signifier of the monstrous which is a feature of Gothic fiction. Examples include Shirley Jackson's *The Haunting of Hill House* (1959) and Tennant's *The Bad Sister*.

The Fires of Bride fruitfully exploits Gothic conventions, while at the same time parodying them. By situating the action on Cailleach, an imaginary location humorously described as 'the outermost island of the Utter Utter Hebrides',[18] Galford gives herself the scope to create an atmospheric and immediately recognizable Gothic landscape, complete with ancient castle, ruined convent and eerily swirling mist. An element of the utopian is apparent in the construction of this milieu since Cailleach, signifying in Gaelic 'the crone', is depicted as a magic world of woman-identified relationships and matriarchal culture. The women living on the island, whose intertwining narratives comprise the text, are described as exceptionally powerful and strong-willed. Galford's approach to lesbianism, like Winterson's, combines lesbian feminist perspectives with present-day critiques. While centering the text on woman-identified relationships and celebrating the courage and imagination of the female characters she portrays, she also highlights their egocentricity and manipulativeness, and playfully exposes the problematic aspects of the lesbian feminist concept of women's community. Cultural feminist ideals of female spirituality and moral superiority are likewise subjected to gentle ridicule.

The text, in representing the adventures of the inhabitants of Cailleach, takes the conventional Gothic form of box within box of interlocking narratives. As in earlier works of fiction structured in this manner, such as Mary Shelley's *Frankenstein* (1818), the characters at the centre of the various narratives, while differing in personality and historical context, all occupy similar roles and positions. As well as being lesbian or woman-identified, they are all writers, artists or mystics. Lizzie, the heroine of the frame narrative, works as a script writer for Caledonian television. She visits Cailleach with the aim of interviewing the natives and producing a feature on the island. Maria, whom she meets in the course of her travels, is an artist and sculptor, while Catriona, the owner of the local castle, is a clan chieftain who dabbles in witchcraft. The hub of these interlocking narratives is Mhairi, an eleventh-century nun. She is a specialist in manuscript illumination and devotes her youth to painstakingly making copies of the Book of Bride, an apocryphal gospel which recounts the life of the female twin of Jesus Christ. The orthodox Roman Catholic Church declares it to be heretical and attempts to prevent its circulation. Mhairi and her sister nuns are punished for the part they play in its production. Mhairi exists less as a fully drawn character than as a symbol of female innocence and woman's capacity to resist oppression. Women's life in the Middle Ages is described as one of hardship, supporting the view that the postmodernist treatment of history is 'critical' rather than 'nostalgic'.[19]

Another feature which the female inhabitants of Cailleach have in common is that they all employ their creative abilities for political ends, using them to challenge patriarchal attitudes and values. And male-dominated society, whether exemplified by the Medieval ecclesiastics who have jurisdiction over Mhairi's convent or by the Calvinist Reverend Murdo MacNeish who seeks to dominate the present-day spiritual life of Cailleach, retaliates in a brutally punitive manner. Galford's emphasis on the function played by art and literature in protesting against misogyny and homophobia develops a theme of importance to the tradition of lesbian writing established by the Lesbian Feminist Movement. It illustrates that, although the narrative strategies favoured by contemporary writers differ from those utilized by their predecessors in the 1970s, the concept of a 'political fiction' continues to flourish.

Sex and the thriller

The interest in sexuality and the exploration of its psychological and cultural implications which was stimulated by the writing of the lesbian sexual radicals in the 1980s and 1990s[20] is not only reflected in theoretical essays[21] and sex magazines[22] but has also had an impact on works of fiction. The genre which responded most quickly to its influence is the *thriller*. In the 1980s a focus on sex was, in fact, a distinctive feature of lesbian crime fiction, differentiating it from lesbian fiction of a more general kind. While writers such as March and Anna Wilson, influenced by lesbian feminist attitudes, were envisaging sexual attraction in terms of identification, concentrating on themes of romance and woman-bonding, and avoiding explicit accounts of sex, thriller writers such as Wings and Forrest were representing desire in terms of difference and introducing descriptions of sexual encounters into their novels. The reason they felt free to write explicitly about sex when other writers apparently did not lies, I suggest, in the area of genre and convention. The thriller has traditionally been regarded as a form of escapist entertainment and examples of it, as is illustrated by the novels of Fleming and Martin Sands, frequently include references to sexual encounters. This gives the thriller writer a licence to focus on sexual practice and fantasy which, in the early and mid-eighties, was denied to writers of other kinds of lesbian fiction. It is one which, with an eye to attracting readers and increasing her sales, she understandably exploits.

However, the references to sex in the lesbian thriller are not merely commercial in aim but serve other purposes too. In some cases they function as metaphors for the conventional concerns of crime detection. Voyeurism and butch-femme identification, two motifs which are particularly popular with lesbian thriller writers, are admirably suited, as we shall see, to the depiction of espionage and disguise.

In employing the thriller as a vehicle for treating sex and the erotic, writers employ a variety of different discourses and approaches. Forrest and Wings, conceptualizing desire in terms of difference and the contraries of dominance/submission, introduce motifs of sexual objectification, 'the look', and codes of dress and behaviour relating to butch-femme role-play. In referring to 'the look', they transgress patriarchal convention by portraying female characters appropriating it. In Forrest's *Amateur City* (1984) Kate, who is attracted to Ellen, stares intently at her, influencing her to move and act self-consciously.[23] In Wings's *She Came Too Late* Emma Victor, gazing appreciatively at Julie Arbeder, notices that 'she had a broad chest and the silk shirt was pulling slightly against her small breasts' (Wings 1986: 13). As this quotation illustrates, the effect of the transgression is certainly not politically radical. Woman continues to be the focus of sexual objectification – though, in this case, she is objectified not by the male gaze but by that of the female character and reader. The look of Kate and Emma carry the narrative forward, and the reader, who is positioned to identify with it, shares in its implications of pleasure and power.

Writers' treatment of the motif of 'the look' varies considerably in sophistication. The use which Wings makes of it is more self-aware and subversive than Forrest's. Introducing an element of pastiche, which is stylishly postmodern, she humorously parodies the macho gaze of the male sleuth and its objectifying focus – as, for example, in Emma's enthusiastic description of her lover Frances Cohen's figure: 'She had real hips, real lady's hips like two holsters hanging below her waist' (p. 37). The passage, by employing cliché and exaggeration, alerts the reader to the contrary brutality/absurdity of male fantasy projections of women.

The motif of 'the look', as employed by Wings and Schulman, frequently carries connotations of voyeurism. Wings utilizes it with exceptional wit in the episode of the strip-show which occurs toward the end of *She Came Too Late*. Emma, in search of a temporary diversion from her sleuthing, enters a Boston nightclub. The strip-show which she witnesses there serves several different functions. As well as exciting her erotically and giving her an opportunity to display her fashionably sexy temperament to the reader, it arouses in her thoughts of biology and procreation which provide the clue to the solution of the crime she is investigating. In addition, the look of complicity which she and the stripper momentarily share has the effect of subverting the heterosexual character of the strip-show and unexpectedly transforming it into a sexual encounter between two women. Emma describes how,

> While the men were busy with her [the stripper's] back, she was looking me squarely in the face. Her eyes gave away her surprise at seeing a woman, sitting alone directly in front of her. Our two faces glowed, but she had all her moves down for the johns behind her and I watched her decide what to do with me. Our mutual realisation was making me fall into a well growing between my legs. She kept going with her routine, putting the feather boa between her legs for the guys behind her, turning around and looking me in the eyes as she drew it through her crotch. (Wings 1986: 180)

In Schulman's *After Delores* the relationship which the anonymous narrator-cum-sleuth forms with Beatriz and Charlotte, the mysteriously glamorous couple with whom she inadvertently becomes involved, and the pleasures which it affords her, are represented by a series of voyeuristic acts. She first encounters the two women in a shabby New York theatre and, on watching them rehearse a love scene together, experiences a disconcerting sense of confusion between life and art. She also savours for the first time the excitement of the role of spy, which she is to play with increasing frequency as her relationship with the couple and her involvement in the role of sleuth develop. Commenting on the incident, she observes:

> It was only when she [Charlotte] had finished that I remembered it wasn't real. I felt like a spy in a private conversation, and when the conversation was over, I had a stake in it. When the actress dropped her hands and stood quietly on the stage I missed the character that she had become, and felt sad to watch her disappear. So, I let myself stay hidden there in the shadows, waiting to be thrilled again. (Schulman, *After Delores*, 1990: 36)

On a subsequent occasion she watches Charlotte and Beatriz through the peephole in the door of their apartment as they enact another love scene. This time they are naked – and their passion is genuine. The sexual thrill which she achieves from playing the role of voyeur is indicated by her description of the peephole as 'cavernous, I could have crawled into it' – and by her reference to the 'sweaty handprints' which she makes while leaning against the door (p. 126). Again she compares herself to a spy; she describes herself as feeling 'like a thief in the night, like a traitor committing espionage' (p. 126).

The writers cited above manifest, it is interesting to note, three different approaches to the theme of dominance/submission and butch–femme identification in sexual relations.[24] Forrest, who appears to envisage sex-roles in essentialist terms, portrays her sleuth Kate Delafield as innately butch. Schulman and Wings, in keeping with the postmodernist style of their fiction, adopt a more intellectually sophisticated approach. The former, employing a psychoanalytic perspective, represents the subject's adoption of a particular position or role as motivated by a set of psychic and cultural structures, the sources of which are too complex to fathom and over which she has little, if any, control. The latter adopts a more frivolous attitude, one which, as befits the commercial consumer society which forms the backdrop to her novels, foregrounds the motifs of 'choice', 'pleasure' and 'play'. She emphasizes the fluidity of lesbian sexual positions and portrays the subject shifting from role to role at will. In *She Came Too Late* and *She Came in a Flash* butch–femme identification is represented largely as a matter of fashion and personal preference. Emma, though generally adopting the androgynous or butch role which has been popular with lesbians since the 1970s, none the less enjoys assuming an exaggeratedly femme disguise when her investigative activities so require. Having attired herself in the seductive ensemble of black dress, black stockings and stiletto heels, Wings's new Eve humorously remarks, irreverently parodying the divine act of creation, 'I saw it was good. I was a girl.'[25] This episode illustrates Wings's ability to combine in an ingenious and amusing manner the motif of disguise, which is conventional to the thriller, with the sexual theme of role-play, and the psychological one of the feminine masquerade.[26] The latter are, of course, key topics in contemporary lesbian/feminist discourse.

Other aspects of sexuality which receive attention in the lesbian thriller are transsexualism and sadomasochism. Barbara Wilson focuses on both. Her approach to transsexualism in *Gaudí Afternoon* (1990) is informative and lively. She concentrates attention on the confusions over identity and the problems of child custody which it can involve. Her treatment of the currently fashionable topic of SM[27] in *The Dog Collar Murders* (1989) is, in my view, less successful. Her analysis of psychology is too superficial and her style of writing too lightweight to be capable of probing the complexities and contradictions which characterize it. However, the novel, while unsuccessful as a study of SM relations, succeeds in conveying to the reader, albeit in a rather simplistic and schematized way, the substance of the debates relating to SM and the different ideological approaches which women adopt towards it.

The Dog Collar Murders hinges on the controversy between feminists who hold men responsible for acts of aggression and violence, and those who believe that women too have aggressive instincts. The former viewpoint is represented by a group of anti-pornography activists led by Loie Marsh, and the latter by Gracie London, a Civil Rights worker, who opposes censorship. Loie and her companions condemn lesbian SM as a vicious and degrading abuse of power carried out by a group of women who are male-identified. Nicky, a practitioner of SM, disagrees with this analysis. She defends SM on the grounds that it enables women to act out, in a controlled and safe manner, their violent fantasies and urge to dominate. This academic debate about 'women and violence' is unexpectedly interrupted by the occurrence of an actual violent deed. Loie is found murdered. She has been strangled by a dog collar, a symbol of the SM Movement. The crime investigation, undertaken by Pam Nilsen, yields a varied assortment of suspects. They include feminists who are opposed to SM, exponents of the practice and Loie's former lover.

Schulman's *After Delores* also focuses on sadomasochistic relations. In contrast to Wilson, Schulman's insight into the realm of sexual fantasy and her disturbing ability to convey the pressures which the unconscious exerts on the individual makes her admirably suited to treating the topic. The novel centres not on the SM Movement *per se* but on the part which sadomasochistic tendencies and syndromes play in personal relationships. The narrator's involvement with her faithless lover Delores illustrates their power. Her state of mind fluctuates alarmingly between a mood of servile dependence and brutal fantasies of smashing Delores's face in and blowing her brains out. Her relationship with Charlotte, the enigmatic actress who enjoys domination, is tinged with a strong element of masochism. The image of power and cruelty which Charlotte projects is, in fact, the essence of her allure. As the narrator masochistically comments, 'There was something so brutal in her smile. She was a very dangerous woman. She could really hurt me. And I realized that I wanted her fingers inside me right then. They were long and rough' (Schulman, *After Delores*, 1990: 85–6). The attraction which this kind of relationship holds for the narrator is clarified by her telling remark: 'I feel close to people when I'm afraid of them' (p. 157).

Another approach which lesbian thriller writers adopt in representing sexual involvements between women is the psychoanalytic discourse of mother/daughter relations in the infant pre-oedipal stage.[28] This relates to the concept of woman–identification and, unlike the discourse associated with butch-femme role-play and sadomasochism, allows for an emphasis on tenderness as well as power.

The importance of the theme of the pre-oedipal to the lesbian thriller has already been noted by critics. Munt, discussing the assault on patriarchal authority figures which typifies the genre, asks the pertinent question: 'I want to know what is the symbolic and psychoanalytic import of "murdering our fathers"? To retrieve that ideal and perfect union with our mothers perhaps . . . is that why I'm reading these books?'[29] Munt's hypothesis that one of the pleasures which the lesbian thriller offers the reader is the analysis of love between women in terms of a displaced version of the mother/daughter bond, is substantiated by reference to particular novels. Andrea Ross, a visitor to the Nightwood Bar in Forrest's thriller of that name, comments on the symbolic importance of the mother/daughter dyad. She describes Dory, the teenage murder victim, as subliminally engaged in 'looking for a mother lover'. She also tentatively suggests, 'I suspect sometimes we're just trying to get back to a safer time when we were our mothers' daughters. Back to when we were children and had no knowledge of men and how much they would control our lives.'[30] This idealized representation of mother/daughter relations as an untroubled haven of tranquillity is rejected by feminist psychoanalysts.[31] It is also contradicted by the actual events of the novel. In portraying Dory's relations with her biological mother, Flora Quillin, and with her surrogate mother, Dr Marietta Hall, Forrest acknowledges the destructive, power-ridden aspect of the mother/daughter attachment as well as the nurturing, loving side.

Wings's *She Came Too Late* also represents relations between women, both sexual and platonic, in terms of a displaced version of the mother/daughter dyad. The investigator Emma admits to feeling 'an unrelenting, silly maternalism' towards Sue, an acquaintance who is hooked on drugs (p. 71). Descriptions of Emma's love relationship with Frances Cohen alternate between images of dominance/subordination verging on the sadomasochistic, and references to maternal nurture. Emma's initial physical encounter with Frances takes the form of a humorous parody of mother/daughter positions. She is pushed against Frances in a crowd of people, loses her balance – and discovers with pleasure and astonishment 'then she was on the floor and I was in her lap!' (p. 6)

Sex and desire

Although the thriller has undoubtedly played a pioneering role in the representation of lesbian sex and fantasy, the treatment of these topics is, of course, no longer the prerogative of this particular genre. In the past few years sex has become an increasingly common theme in lesbian fiction. While this trend is chiefly associated with North America, British texts have also contributed to it – as is illustrated by the two collections of lesbian erotic writing *Serious Pleasure* (1989) and *More Serious Pleasure* (1990), published by Sheba Collective, and by Winterson's *Written on the Body* (1992).

Written on the Body recounts the sexual adventures of a narrator whose gender is unstated. The style is more obviously derivative than that of Winterson's other novels for, while all her writing displays an intertextual focus, here the allusions to works by other writers appear at times untransformed by imagination. The descriptions of sex and the analyses of its philosophical implications which occur in the text read on occasion like a British version of Wittig's *The Lesbian Body* (1973) – spiced with a pungent element of seventeenth-century Metaphysical wit and conceit.

The novel's treatment of sexual experience offers few new insights but tends to reproduce the perceptions of earlier writers. Emphasis falls predictably on the shifting nature of desire and the irrational deeds and acts of psychological cruelty which it prompts the individual to commit. Obsessively involved with the mysterious Louise, the narrator loses interest in her/his former lovers and treats them unnecessarily callously. Focus is also placed on the destructive possessiveness of love and on the frustrations to which the relationship between the self and the Other gives rise. Although the narrator insists, employing imagery reminscent of John Donne, that 'I didn't only want Louise's flesh, I wanted her bones, her blood, her tissues, the sinews that bound her together',[32] total union between lover and beloved is, she discovers, impossible. Louise remains as autonomous and unfathomable as ever.

The utilization of a narrator whose gender is undeclared, the feature of the novel which has aroused most critical attention, is no mere gimmick but serves an important ideological function. It enables Winterson to avoid focusing on a specific sexual identification and, in keeping with the perspectives of Queer Politics,[33] to challenge the conventional division between homosexuality and heterosexuality. The passages of sexual description are open to alternative readings, either lesbian or heterosexual.

However, the device also involves her in difficulties and helps to explain the novel's limitations. One of the most powerful aspects of her writing is the vivid descriptions of location. These include the real and the surreal, ranging from the market in *Oranges Are Not the Only Fruit*, with its stalls and colourful characters, to the fantastic city in *Sexing the Cherry* where 'men and women in balloons fly up and, armed with mops and scrubbing brushes, do battle with the canopy of words' (Winterson 1990: 17). In this novel, however, there are few such descriptions. The lover's body, whether beautiful, as in the early chapters, or envisaged as a skeleton in the later ones is the sole object of interest and everything else is seen as superfluous. As the narrator, obsessed with Louise, rhetorically asks, 'What other places are there in the world than those discovered on a lover's body?' The novel's narrowness of focus stems, however, not so much from the subject matter as from the writing. As Donne's *Songs and Sonnets* amply illustrate, love's miraculous ability to 'make one little room an everywhere' does not necessarily preclude reference to other geographical areas and spheres.

Although British writers have made some contribution to the fictional delineation of lesbian perspectives on sex, it is at the moment a relatively minor one. It is American writers who provide the most original and multifaceted accounts. Barbara Wilson's *Cows and Horses* (1986) and De-Lynn's *Don Juan in the Village* (1990) furnish pertinent and thought-provoking examples.

Cows and Horses interrogates the concept of erotic attraction as 'difference', while also teasing out the contradictions relating to desire. The protagonist Bet, who has always disliked the idea of role-play, unexpectedly finds herself attracted to Kelly, an impulsive and self-centred butch. A conversation at the centre of the novel introduces a discussion about butch-femme identification which both articulates the themes which it treats and provides a frame for their analysis. Attention is focused on the lack of a suitable language to describe lesbian sex and the roles and positions which partners adopt. One of the women portrayed humorously suggests substituting the terms 'apples and oranges' for 'butch and femme', in order to avoid the judgemental attitudes associated with the latter. An argument ensues about whether the individual's adoption of a particular role depends on psychology, socialization, body movements or dress. The suggestion is voiced that sex-roles have nothing to do with any of these factors but depend on the interaction between the two partners – 'the fact that they're attracted to each other'.[34] This agrees with Case's theory that the butch-femme couple has to be seen as a duo whose roles and positions are defined solely in relation to one another.[35] Bet's sadly voiced question, 'I wonder why we divide it all up, when we could have so much more, we could have the whole thing?', is at odds with contemporary attitudes and meets with an unsympathetic response. It encounters the brisk rejoinder, 'Because people think it's sexy!' (p. 74).

Like *Cows and Horses*, some of the stories in DeLynn's *Don Juan in the Village* treat the theme of butch-femme identification. However, the collection as a whole has less in common with Wilson's novel than it does with the work of Schulman, another writer discussed in this chapter. Though less political in emphasis, it displays a number of interesting affinities with it.

One crucial link between the texts of DeLynn and Schulman is the focus which they place on the relationship between sex and fantasy. The two writers interrogate the roles and identifications which lovers adopt and the images which they project on one another. They also investigate, in some detail, the fantasy scenarios which they create. Influenced by Queer Politics, both refer to a wide spectrum of different sexual positions and orientations – butch, femme, SM, gay, bisexual, transsexual, lesbian and heterosexual. They also, on occasion, attempt to break down the division between these positions and subvert the conventional homosexual/heterosexual dichotomy by portraying women who identify as lesbian engaging in sexual relations with men – in Schulman's case with a gay man.[36] Episodes of this kind, again in consonance with Queer attitudes, challenge the concept of a unitary stable sexual identity and highlight the fluid and shifting nature of desire.

In addition, both writers appear fascinated by the complexities of sexual fantasy and by the contradictions and conundrums of sex and gender. Kate, one of the characters in Schulman's *People in Trouble*, is first portrayed standing in a department store buying a gift of two bras for her lover Molly. Absentmindedly fingering the material, she constructs a vivid erotic fantasy centering on the contrasting images of femininity (virginal/whorish) they will confer on her. This fantasy serves the purpose of introducing us to Kate's involvement with Molly. It functions, so to speak, as the 'staging' and *mise en scène* for her desire.[37] The fact that the shop assistant, assuming her to be heterosexual, thinks that she is buying the bras for herself ('You'd better try them on. They are too big for you miss', she advises her) highlights both the privacy of Kate's fantasy and, in the respect that it conflicts with the expectations of the dominant culture, its transgressive nature.

References to the contradictions of sex and gender occur frequently in the work of the two writers. While Schulman represents the bisexual Kate dressing in a style which is more overtly butch than the lesbian Molly, DeLynn depicts the narrator of the Epilog to *Don Juan in the Village* asking herself the embarrassing question if she were not 'really . . . a man in a woman's body, perhaps a redneck man in a woman's body, or maybe something even worse – a man who liked to fuck men in a woman's body' (DeLynn 1991: 237). The quotation illustrates the part which gender displacements play in sexual fantasy and comments, somewhat ruefully, on the lack of control which the subject has over the identifications which she adopts.

The episodes cited above typify Schulman's and DeLynn's perspectives on sex. They reject the concept of a simple lesbian and bisexual identity – and highlight how imprecise and crass these labels are as definitions of our sexual orientations and identifications. As well as drawing attention to the diverse and idiosyncratic positions and subjectivities which the labels encompass and conceal, they indicate (especially in the case of the quotation from DeLynn's Epilog) the intricate and often tortuous routes which we take to arrive at them. They not only acknowledge the important role which fantasy plays in sexual relations but also come close to endorsing Lacan's observation that its significance is, in fact, paramount. Since all the relationships which we form depend on imaginary projections and images, 'the whole of [our] realisation in the sexual relation comes down to fantasy.'[38]

The stories in DeLynn's *Don Juan in the Village*, in addition to exploring the connections between sex and fantasy, also investigate different social and ethnic constructs of lesbianism. The visits which the New York narrator pays to different cities and countries function as a pretext to explore these constructs, along with the power structures they reflect. While holidaying in San Juan, Puerto Rico, she visits the local gay bar with the aim, as she patronizingly puts it, of 'fraternizing with the natives' (p. 17). The event, however, turns out to be less of a success than she had anticipated. The habitués of the bar practice an extreme form of role-play, the butches attired in dark suits and the femmes in low-cut dresses and high-heels. They strike the narrator as totally alien – and have nothing in common with her friends at home. They remind her nostalgically and disturbingly of the women whom she used to know in the early 1970s before the advent of the Lesbian Feminist Movement outlawed role-play as politically incorrect. The Puerto Rican lesbians are apparently no more impressed by her than she is by them – and they express their disdain by ostracizing her and refusing to talk. After meeting with similar treatment at the other bars in the area, she is unwillingly forced to acknowledge the fact of 'difference'. She is, she perceives, 'an outsider in their world, as they are in mine' (p. 32).

'Butch', another story in the collection, also focuses on the dynamics of role-play, and on the social and psychological contradictions which it can involve. The middle-class narrator, on picking up a working-class butch in a New York bar, treats her in a contemptuous and humiliating manner. On leaving the bar, she even insists that her new companion walk behind her in case her friends see them together and accuse her of 'slumming'. Once the two are in bed, however, the roles are reversed. The narrator accepts her butch partner's domination and submits, with a paradoxical mixture of curiosity and disgust, pleasure and pain, to the practices to which she is subjected.

Romance / anti-romance

The narrator of the Epilog to DeLynn's *Don Juan in the Village,* looking back on the early years of the Gay Liberation Movement, remembers envying the gay men she knew their sexual adventurousness and willing-ness to experiment with new partners, while feeling impatient with her fellow lesbians for requiring 'romantic justification' (p. 236) for engaging in sexual relations. Ironically, she herself appears to have suffered from similar inhibitions since she admits that the only way she could bring herself to fancy someone was by convincing herself that she was no ordinary mortal but 'the most desirable [woman] in the world' (p. 237). The account which she gives of the adventures embarked on by herself and her male com-panions focuses on the part which fantasy identifications and scenarios play in sexual relations. It also mingles romantic perceptions with anti-romantic ones. She portrays herself cruising the city in the role of 'James Dean, a cowboy coming off a dusty plain' (p. 236) and, creating an exotic mélange of sacred and profane imagery resembling Djuna Barnes's *Nightwood* (1937), transforms the broken-down pier where the gay men used to hold their assignations into an

> unholy cathedral, one in which the scent was of marijuana and pop-pers rather than incense, the offering not wine and wafers but the white droppings of birds and men: the latter of which was absorbed by kneeling bodies in a mystic transformation of Idea into Flesh. (p. 236)

It is difficult to assess the precise tone of this description. The element of rhetorical excess and the richness of the imagery imply a note of parody, suggesting that the narrator intends it as an ironic comment on her earlier romantic self. The grimly cryptic allusion to AIDS which follows – 'And how could anyone know that amidst the dark, warm, moist lushness of herpes, clap, amebiasis, hepatitis, syphilis, crabs, etc., other transformations were taking place too?' – also suggests a critique of the romantic attitudes to sex current in the 1970s.

The interplay between romantic and anti-romantic perspectives, which occurs in this passage, is typical of DeLynn's writing and that of certain of her contemporaries, Schulman in particular. Fortunate heirs to a rich tradi-tion of lesbian romantic fiction,[39] present-day writers feel free to appropri-ate its structures and motifs while simultaneously questioning and subverting the sentiments which they express. As a result, romantic and anti-romantic strands interact in a number of contemporary texts, contend-ing for dominance. DeLynn and Schulman intersperse and juxtapose them with poignancy and wit.

DeLynn's 'Night Diving' (*Don Juan in the Village,* 1990) illustrates one strategy employed by writers to interweave romantic and anti-romantic elements. The story focuses on a holiday love affair in the Caribbean, and references to the allure of the sea constitute a seductive refrain. The narrator challenges the heterosexist attitudes of the diving party of which she is a member by Coming Out to a fellow holiday-maker – and the reader is even treated to the thrill of an under-water kiss. However, the romantic connotations of these motifs is sharply undercut by their cynical and ribald treatment. The narrator, a sophisticated New Yorker, makes a pass at her diving partner Beryl, not because she is in love with her, but prompted by the questionable motives of lust and a desire to shock. The Coming Out episode is, in fact, a comic parody of the kind which appears in the lesbian romances of the 1970s. Beryl, revealing the prejudices instilled in her by her provincial upbringing, initially refuses to believe the narrator's assertion that she is lesbian. She has doubts about the existence of lesbians altogether for, as she naively remarks, to her knowledge 'there are no homosexuals in Saskatoon' (p. 200). This crass display of ignorance provokes the narrator into employing cruder methods to convince her; she stares at her cleavage 'in a theatrical over-dramatized fashion . . . as if I were a guy' (p. 199). Her approach to Beryl, far from being romantic, is insensitive and coarse, endorsing the stereotype of the predatory lesbian.

'Night Diving', while undercutting the popular motif of the holiday romance, also challenges the romantic idea that love and intimate relation-ships constitute the touchstone of identity and personal fulfilment. The narrator has no illusions about her feelings for Beryl. She recognizes that they are motivated by a sexual desire which leads her to behave foolishly and irresponsibly. As she wryly observes, 'The serpent entered paradise; it always does: the serpent of sex and knowledge' (p. 195). The sense of existential freedom which she experiences when exploring the ocean depths on diving expeditions is represented as more emotionally fulfilling than the sordid sex adventures which she pursues when on the land. In comparison with 'the pure and simple happiness' to be achieved from 'the rapture of the deep' (pp. 221, 222), sexual involvements, whether lesbian or heterosexual, emerge from the story as tainted and compromised.

Whereas the interplay between romantic and anti-romantic elements in DeLynn's fiction is relatively narrow in scope, centering on the individual or the couple, in Schulman's it is considerably wider. It relates to the interests of the gay community as a whole and has a marked political dimension. *People in Trouble*, Schulman's most complex and compelling work to date, probes the contradiction of the individual focusing her ener-gies on personal relationships when, all around her, people are suffering from extreme poverty or dying from AIDS. This contradiction is summed up in a remark which Molly makes to her married lover Kate when, strolling through New York City together, they find what they had in-tended to be an intimate tête à tête frequently interrupted by pleas for help from the destitute passers-by: 'Here we are trying to have a run-of-the-mill illicit lesbian love affair . . . and all around us people are dying and asking for money.'[40] Molly's comment, and the strategies which Schulman employs to convey its import to the reader, not only question the value of personal relationships but also problematize the genre of the lesbian romance itself. The AIDS crisis, Schulman implies, is of such immense significance and reveals such a vast abyss of suffering and social injustice that it challenges traditional forms of fiction, making the conventional romance, with its privileging of the personal and the sentimental, appear inappropriate and outmoded. As she comments in a recent interview, 'A major theme in *People in Trouble* is that it has become impossible to write a gay book without discussing AIDS in some detail.'[41]

The interaction between personal and political dimensions of experience, between a romance narrative and the anti-romantic references to poverty and death which undercut it, is established in the opening pages of the novel. We move abruptly from the apocalyptic statement, 'It was the beginning of the end of the world but not everyone noticed right away' (Schulman, *People in Trouble*, 1990: 1), to the description of Kate fantasizing about Molly's breasts as she stands in a New York store buying her a gift of lingerie. The episode illustrates how, unaware of or unmoved by the suffering which is taking place a few blocks away, people continue to concentrate on personal concerns, buying presents for their lovers and indulging in erotic fantasies.

People in Trouble achieves the feat of modifying the structures of the lesbian romance in response to the AIDS crisis. As well as examining the connections between personal and political areas of life, it explores the process of radicalization which the individual experiences as a result of working with people with AIDS. In order to illustrate this, the second half of the novel moves away from a focus on individual characters and their relationships and concentrates on the activities of the lesbian and gay community as a whole.

The themes and narrative strategies discussed above, though innovatory from the point of view of the lesbian fiction published in the late 1980s and the 1990s, appear, when placed in the context of contemporary feminist fiction in general, notably more traditional. In terms of structure, *People in Trouble* reveals affinities with certain radical feminist novels published in the 1970s and early 1980s. Piercy's *Small Changes* (1972) and *Braided Lives* (1982), and Marilyn French's *The Women's Room* (1977), as I illustrate elsewhere,[42] portray the individual becoming politically radicalized, and move in the later chapters to a focus on the group and its activities – the commune movement and the abortion network in Piercy's novels and the radical feminist collective in French's. Schulman's novel reflects a similarly centrifugal movement. It depicts Molly and Kate becoming increasingly politically aware and highlights, in the second half, the activities of 'Justice', an organization formed with the aim of fighting the hypocrisy surrounding the AIDS epidemic and protecting the rights of people with AIDS. The novel's pessimistic and open-ended conclusion – 'Some deaths are shocking, some invisible. We are a people in trouble. We do not act' (p. 228) is more depressing than those of Piercy's novels but strikes a similarly bleak note to *The Women's Room*. One of the achievements of *People in Trouble* is, thus, to bring together old and new perceptions and structures. It adventurously attempts to combine certain features associated with postmodernism, such as the representation of society in a state of fragmentation and flux, an analysis of sexual fantasy and an emphasis on different sexual identifications, with a sense of political commitment and an emphasis on the community reminiscent of the feminist perspectives of the 1970s. The vitality of the novel depends partly, in fact, on the tension between these contrary impulses and interests.

Like other texts discussed in this chapter, such as Galford's *The Fires of Bride, People in Trouble* discusses the function played by art and literature in sexual politics. Kate is an artist and, influenced by Molly's involvement in the AIDS crisis, she shifts in the course of the narrative from a liberal position in which, though sympathetic to the suffering taking place around her, she sees it as irrelevant to her artistic interests, to adopting a more radical stance. On learning that novels have been written on the topic of AIDS, she decides to utilize her art to make a political statement. The project which she chooses, self-reflexively entitled 'People in Trouble', meets with ridicule and criticism from the postmodernist New York art clique. A gallery owner pretentiously disparages it on the grounds that it lacks 'pictorial entrapment' and 'archetectonic space' (p. 197), while her husband accuses its subject matter of being narrow and 'exclusive' (p. 127). The latter's unsympathetic response is not unbiased but reflects feelings of resentment towards Kate for becoming involved in a lesbian relationship. As on other occasions in the novel, the individual's judgements are shown to be coloured and distorted by personal emotion and self-interest.

While strongly affirming the political importance of cultural practice, *People in Trouble* simultaneously acknowledges the ridicule and misunderstanding which a political emphasis in art and literature is likely to encounter today. Schulman's approach to the topic, like her view of the individual's relationship with society and her/his power to influence public attitudes, is clear-sighted and by no means complacent. The novel illustrates both the difficulties which the lesbian writer faces in attempting to create political fiction in the era of the 1990s, and some of the strategies which she employs to surmount them.

As this study illustrates, over the past two decades lesbian writing has become a flourishing literary form, one which is notable for its intellectual and stylistic diversity. Although predictions in this area have to be viewed with caution, it is interesting to contemplate the direction which it will take in the future.

The sign *lesbian* is, in the 1990s, the pivot of conflicting ideologies and attitudes – and with the current wave of homophobia occurring in the United Kingdom and North America, the outcome of the struggle for liberation waged by lesbians and gay men is by no means clear. Will lesbian writing continue to make a contribution to this struggle by treating political themes, as Galford's and Schulman's novels do, or will writers and theorists increasingly take refuge in topics and discourses of an esoteric, elitist kind? Will lesbian theory proliferate and diversify with the speed with which it has in recent years? Will theorists find a means to reconcile and bring together the interests of politics/pleasure, activism/academia, and identification/difference, which, at the moment, are generally regarded as conflicting and incompatible?

And what about the future of lesbian fiction? Will the assimilation of lesbian themes into women's fiction in general, which, as is illustrated by the novels of Margaret Atwood and Fay Weldon, is starting to take place,[43] have the effect of making lesbian fiction as a specific category redundant and cause it, having served its political purpose, to disappear? Judging from the oppressive climate which at present characterizes lesbian and gay life on both sides of the Atlantic, such an event is unlikely – as a short-term prospect, at least. In fact, both the political function which lesbian fiction serves in making lesbianism culturally visible and the current emphasis in Lesbian Studies on the specificity of the sign *lesbian* (as distinct from *woman* and *feminist*), ensure that, while some degree of interaction will certainly continue to take place between 'lesbian fiction' and 'women's fiction', the former will remain, in the foreseeable future, a separate category.

However, while we may safely predict that lesbian fiction will continue to exist, the precise form which it will take and the characteristics it will display give scope for speculation. A distinctive feature of contemporary lesbian novels and stories, as many of the works discussed above illustrate, is the interplay which they create between narrative and theory. Will writers continue to enrich their texts by appropriating and reworking ideas from theoretical discourse? Will fantasy themes and postmodern strategies of the kind employed by Galford, Winterson and Wings, remain in fashion, or will there be a return to the realist mode of writing which was popular in the 1970s? Or will these different styles continue to co-exist, highlighting the varied nature of lesbian fiction and offering the reader an element of choice, as is the case at present? Will popular genres such as the thriller and the comic novel, which treat issues relating to sexual politics in an accessible, lively format, continue to entertain and empower readers?

These are some of the questions which contemporary lesbian writing raises. They have political as well as cultural significance – and will no doubt be pondered and discussed by readers in years to come.

Notes

1 Zimmerman, *The Safe Sea of Women*, ed. cit., pp. 207–24.
2 Zimmerman, *The Safe Sea of Women*, ed. cit., p. 216.
3 The topic is treated in Jan Clausen, *Mother, Sister, Daughter, Lover: Stories* (Women's Press, 1981) and Roberts's *A Piece of the Night*, ed. cit.
4 For reference to feminism and postmodernism see Linda Hutcheon, *The Politics of Postmodernism* (Routledge, 1989), pp. 141–68.
5 Winterson, *Oranges Are Not the Only Fruit*, ed. cit., p. 93.
6 Zimmerman expresses this view in *The Safe Sea of Women*, ed. cit., pp. 209–10.
7 For reference to the problems experienced by lesbian and gay teenagers, see McKenna's feature in *The Guardian* cited in Chapter 1, note 22.
8 Duncker, *Sisters and Strangers*, ed. cit., p. 191.
9 Winterson, 'Foreword', *Oranges Are Not the Only Fruit* (Vintage, 1991), xiii.
10 Cixous, 'Sorties', *New French Feminisms*, ed. cit., p. 97.
11 See Joyce McDougall, *Theatres of the Mind: Illusion and Truth on the Psychoanalytic Stage* (Free Association Books, 1986).
12 Cixous, 'Sorties', ed. cit., p. 97.
13 Jonathan Culler, *On Deconstruction: Theory and Criticism after Structuralism* (Routledge and Kegan Paul, 1983), pp. 134–9.
14 Hutcheon, op. cit., pp. 50–1.
15 *Lady Oracle* (1976; Virago, 1982).
16 Winterson, *Sexing the Cherry* (Vintage, 1990), p. 90.
17 See Zimmerman, 'Lesbians Like This and That', ed. cit., p. 4.
18 Galford, *The Fires of Bride,* ed. cit., p. 5.
19 Hutcheon, op. cit., p. 93.
20 For reference to this see Chapter 2, pp. 22–28.
21 See Vance, *Pleasure and Danger*, ed. cit.
22 Examples include the American publications *On Our Backs* and *Bad Attitudes*, both of which originated in 1984. For reference to them, see Faderman, *Odd Girls*, ed. cit., p. 258.
23 Pandora edition, p. 60.
24 These different approaches are discussed in Chapter 2, pp. 27–28.
25 Wings, *She Came Too Late*, ed. cit., p. 90.
26 See the essays by Stephen Heath and Joan Riviere in Victor Burgin, James Donald and Cora Kaplan (eds) *Formations of Fantasy* (Methuen, 1986), pp. 35–61.
27 See Chapter 2, pp. 25–27.
28 See Ryan, 'Psychoanalysis and Women Loving Women', ed. cit., pp. 196–209.
29 'The Inverstigators', ed. cit., p. 106.
30 Forrest, *Murder at the Nightwood Bar,* ed. cit., p. 31.

31 See Judith Kegan Gardiner, 'Mind Mother: Psychoanalysis and Feminism', in *Making a Difference*, ed. cit., pp. 113–45.

32 Winterson, *Written on the Body* (Jonathan Cape, 1992), p. 51.

33 Theorists base the deconstruction of the homosexual/heterosexual dichotomy on a radical reading of Freud's theory of polymorphous perversity. For reference to their ideas, see Maggie Davis's feature on Queer Politics in *The Pink Paper*, 21 February 1993, p. 10; and Jonathan Dollimore's essay in Joseph Bristow, ed., *Sexual Sameness: Textual Differences in Lesbian and Gay Writing* (Routledge, 1992), pp. 9–25.

34 Barbara Wilson, *Cows and Horses* (Virago, 1989), p. 72. Subsequent references are to this edition and in the text.

35 For reference to Case's 'Toward a Butch-Femme Aesthetic', see Chapter 2, p. 30.

36 See DeLynn, *Don Juan in the Village*, ed. cit., pp. 29, 100; and Schulman, *Girls, Visions and Everything*, ed. cit., p. 143.

37 See Elizabeth Cowie, 'Fantasia', in Parveen Adams and Cowie, (eds) *The Woman in Question: m/f* (Verso, 1990), p. 149.

38 Lacan, quoted in Juliet Mitchell and Jacqueline Rose (eds) *Feminine Sexuality: Jacques Lacan and the Ecole Freudienne* (Macmillan, 1982).

39 For reference to the lesbian romance, see Diane Hamer, '"I am a Woman": Ann Bannon and the Writing of Lesbian Identity in the 1950s', in *Lesbian and Gay Writing*, ed. cit., pp. 47–75; and Joke Hermes, 'Sexuality in Lesbian Romance Fiction', *Feminist Review*, 42 (1992), pp. 49–66.

40 Schulman, *People in Trouble*, ed. cit., p. 113.

41 Schulman, 'Troubled Times', in Betsy Warland (ed.) *Inversions: Writings by Dykes, Queers and Lesbians* (Open Letters, 1992), p. 219.

42 Palmer, *Contemporary Women's Fiction*, ed. cit., pp. 48–50, 133, 148–50.

43 I discuss the representations of lesbianism in the fiction of Atwood, Weldon and Angela Carter, and their political implications in 'Contemporary Lesbian Feminist Fiction: Texts for Everywoman', ed. cit., pp. 59–62.

Bibliography

Novels and Stories

Alther, Lisa, *Kinflicks* (New York, Knopf, 1976; Harmondsworth, Penguin, 1977).

Alther, Lisa, *Other Women* (New York, Knopf, 1984; Harmondsworth, Penguin, 1985).

Arnold, June, *Sister Gin* (Plainfield, VT, Daughters Publishing, 1975; London, Women's Press, 1979).

Atwood, Margaret, *Lady Oracle* (Toronto, McClelland and Stewart, 1976; London, Virago, 1982).

Barnes, Djuna, *Nightwood* (London, Faber and Faber, 1936).

Brown, Rita Mae, *Ruby Fruit Jungle* (Plainfield, VT, Daughters Publishing, 1973; London, Corgi, 1978).

Burford, Barbara, *The Threshing Floor* (London, Sheba, 1986).

Carter, Angela, *The Magic Toyshop* (London, Heinemann, 1967; London, Virago, 1981).

Clausen, Jan, *Mother, Sister, Daughter, Lover: Stories* (Trumansberg, NY, Crossing Press, 1980; London, Women's Press, 1981).

Cross, Amanda, *No Word from Winifred* (New York, E.P. Dutton, 1986; London, Virago, 1987).

DeLynn, Jane, *Don Juan in the Village* (New York, Pantheon, 1990; London, Serpent's Tail, 1991).

Doyle, Sir Arthur Conan, *The Hound of the Baskervilles* (London, Newnes, 1902: Harmondsworth, Penguin, 1981).

Du Maurier, Daphne, *Rebecca* (London, Gollancz, 1938).

Forrest, Katherine V., *Daughters of a Coral Dawn* (Tallahassee, FL, Naiad, 1984).

Forrest, Katherine V., *Amateur City* (Tallahassee, FL, Naiad, 1984; London, Pandora, 1987).

Forrest, Katherine V., *Murder at the Nightwood Bar* (Tallahassee, FL, Naiad, 1987; London, Pandora, 1987).

French, Marilyn, *The Women's Room* (New York, Summit, 1977; London, Sphere, 1978).

Galford, Ellen, *The Fires of Bride* (London, Women's Press, 1986).

Galford, Ellen, *Queendom Come* (London, Virago, 1990).

Gearhart, Sally Miller, *The Wanderground: Stories of the Hill Women* (Watertown, MA, Persephone Press, 1979; London, Women's Press, 1985).

Gomez, Jewelle, 'No Day Too Long', in Elly Bulkin (ed.) *Lesbian Fiction: An Anthology* (Massachusetts, Persephone Press, 1981), pp. 219–25.

Grafton, Sue, *A is for Alien* (New York, Holt, Rinehart and Winston, 1982; London, Papermac, 1988).

Harvey, John, *Lonely Hearts* (London, Viking, 1989).

Jackson, Shirley, *The Haunting of Hill House* (New York, Viking, 1959).

James, P.D., *Devices and Desires* (London, Faber, 1989).

Leaton, Anne, *Good Friends, Just* (London, Chatto and Windus, 1988).

Livia, Anna, *Relatively Norma* (London, Onlywomen, 1982).

Livia, Anna, *Bulldozer Rising* (London, Onlywomen, 1988).

McConnell, Vicki P., *Mrs Porter's Letter* (Tallahassee, FL, Naiad, 1982).

McConnell, Vicki P., *The Burnton Widows* (Tallahassee, FL, Naiad, 1984).

McGregor, Iona, *Death Wore a Diadem* (London, Women's Press, 1989).

March, Caeia, *Three Ply Yarn* (London, Women's Press, 1986).

Namjoshi, Suniti, *The Conversations of Cow* (London, Women's Press, 1985).

Oosthuizen, Ann, *Loneliness and Other Lovers* (London, Sheba, 1981).

O'Rourke, Rebecca, *Jumping the Cracks* (London, Virago, 1987).

Paretsky, Sara, *Indemnity Only* (New York, Dial, 1982; Harmondsworth, Penguin, 1986).

Piercy, Marge, *Small Changes* (New York, Doubleday, 1972; New York, Fawcett, 1974).

Piercy, Marge, *The High Cost of Living* (New York, Harper and Row, 1978; London, Women's Press, 1979).

Piercy, Marge, *Braided Lives* (New York, Summit, 1982; Harmondsworth, Penguin, 1983).

Powell, Deborah, *Bayou City Secrets* (Tallahassee, Naiad, 1992; London, Women's Press, 1992).

Rendell, Ruth, *A Demon in My View* (London, Hutchinson, 1976).

Riley, Elizabeth, *All That False Instruction* (London, Angus and Robertson, 1975; London, Sirius Quality Paperback, 1981).

Roberts, Michèle, *A Piece of the Night* (London, Women's Press, 1978).

Russ, Joanna, *The Female Man* (New York, Bantam, 1975; London, Women's Press, 1985).

Russ, Joanna, *On Strike Against God* (USA, Out and Out Books, 1980; London, Women's Press, 1987).

Sarton, May, *A Reckoning* (New York, W.W. Norton, 1978; London, Women's Press, 1984).

Schulman, Sarah, *After Delores* (New York, E.P. Dutton, 1988; London, Sheba, 1990).

Schulman, Sarah, *Girls, Visions and Everything* (Seattle, Seal Press, 1986; London, Sheba, 1991).

Schulman, Sarah, *People in Trouble* (New York, E.P. Dutton, 1990; London, Sheba, 1990).

Scoppettone, Sandra, *Everything You Have is Mine* (Boston, MA, Little, Brown and Company, 1991; London, Virago, 1992).

Scott, Jody, *I, Vampire* (New York, Ace, 1984; London, Women's Press, 1986).

Sheba Collective (ed.) *Serious Pleasure: Lesbian Erotic Stories and Poetry* (London, Sheba, 1989).

Sheba Collective (ed.) *More Serious Pleasure: Lesbian Erotic Stories and Poetry* (London, Sheba, 1990).

Shelley, Mary, *Frankenstein* (1818: Oxford, Oxford University Press, 1969).

Tennant, Emma, *The Bad Sister* (London, Gollancz, 1978; London, Picador, 1979).

Toder, Nancy, *Choices* (Watertown, MA, Persephone Press, 1980).

Wilson, Anna, *Cactus* (London, Onlywomen, 1980).

Wilson, Anna, *Altogether Elsewhere* (London, Onlywomen, 1985).

Wilson, Barbara, *Ambitious Women* (New York, Spinsters Ink, 1982; London, Women's Press, 1983).

Wilson, Barbara, *Murder in the Collective* (Seattle, WA, Seal Press, 1984; London, Women's Press, 1984).

Wilson, Barbara, *Sisters of the Road* (Seattle, WA, Seal Press, 1986; London, Women's Press, 1987).

Wilson, Barbara, *Cows and Horses* (Portland, OR, Eighth Mountain Press, 1988; London, Virago, 1989).

Wilson, Barbara, *The Dog Collar Murders* (Seattle, WA, Seal Press, 1989; London, Virago, 1989).

Wilson, Barbara, *Gaudí Afternoon* (Seattle, WA, Seal Press, 1990; London, Virago, 1991).

Wings, Mary, *She Came Too Late* (London, Women's Press, 1986).

Wings, Mary, *She Came in a Flash* (London, Women's Press, 1988).

Wings, Mary, *Divine Victim* (London, Women's Press, 1992).

Winterson, Jeanette, *Oranges Are Not the Only Fruit* (London, Pandora, 1985; London, Vintage, 1991).

Winterson, Jeanette, *Sexing the Cherry* (London, Bloomsbury, 1989; London, Vintage, 1990).

Winterson, Jeanette, *Written on the Body* (London, Jonathan Cape, 1992).

Wittig, Monique, *The Lesbian Body*, translated by David LeVay (New York, Avon, 1975). (*Le Corps Lesbien*, Paris, Minuit, 1973).

Wittig, Monique, and Zeig, Sande, *Lesbian Peoples: Materials for a Dictionary*, translated by Wittig and Zeig (London, Virago, 1980). (*Brouillon Pour un Dictionaire Des Amantes*, Paris, Grasset & Fasquelle, 1976).

Theoretical and critical works

Ardill, Susan, and O'Sullivan, Sue, 'Upsetting an Applecart: Difference, Desire and Lesbian Sadomasochism', *Feminist Review*, 23 (1986), pp. 31–57.

Ardill, Susan, and O'Sullivan, Sue, 'Butch/Femme Obsessions', *Feminist Review*, 34 (1990), pp. 79–85.

Atkinson, Ti-Grace, 'Lesbianism and Feminism', in Phyllis Birkby, Bertha Harris, Jill Johnston, Esther Newton, Jane O'Wyatt (eds) *Amazon Expedition: A Lesbian Feminist Anthology* (Albion, CA, Times Change Press, 1973), pp. 11–14.

Bakhtin, Mikhail, *Rabelais and his World*, translated by Helene Iswolsky (Cambridge, MA, MIT Press, 1968).

Bakhtin, Mikhail, *Problems of Dostoevsky's Poetics*, translated by Caryl Emerson (Manchester, Manchester University Press, 1984).

Beauvoir, Simone de, *The Second Sex*, translated by H.M. Parshley (Harmondsworth, Penguin, 1972) (*Le Deuxieme Sexe*, Paris, Gallimard, 1949).

Benjamin, Jessica, *The Bonds of Love: Psychoanalysis, Feminism and the Problem of Domination* (New York, Pantheon, 1988).

Benjamin, Jessica, 'Master and Slave: The Fantasy of Erotic Domination', in Ann Snitow, Christine Stansell and Sharon Thompson (eds) *Desire: The Politics of Sexuality* (London, Virago, 1984), pp. 292–311.

Birkby, Phyllis, Harris, Bertha, Johnston, Jill, Newton, Esther, and O'Wyatt, Jane (eds) *Amazon Expedition: A Lesbian Feminist Anthology* (New York, Times Change Press, 1973).

Blackman, Inge, and Perry, Kathryn, 'Skirting the Issue: Lesbian Fashion for the 1990s', *Feminist Review*, 34 (1990), pp. 67–78.

Boucher, Sandy, 'Lesbian Artists', *Heresies*, 3 (1977), p. 43.

Bunch, Charlotte, 'Not for Lesbians Only', in Charlotte Bunch and Gloria Steinem (eds) *Building Feminist Theory: Essays from Quest* (New York, Longman, 1981), pp. 67–73.

Butler, Judith, *Gender Trouble: Feminism and the Subversion of Identity* (London, Routledge, 1990).

Butler, Judith, 'Imitation and Gender Insubordination', in Diana Fuss (ed.) *Inside Out: Lesbian Theories, Gay Theories* (London, Routledge, 1991), pp. 13–31.

Carr, Helen (ed.) *From My Guy to Sci-Fi: Genre and Women's Writing in the Postmodern World* (London, Pandora, 1989).

Cartledge, Sue, and Hemmings, Susan, 'How Did We Get This Way?', in Marsha Rowe (ed.) *Spare Rib Reader* (Harmondsworth, Penguin, 1982), pp. 326–35.

Case, Sue-Ellen, 'Toward a Butch-Femme Aesthetic', in Lynda Hart (ed.) *Making a Spectacle: Feminist Essays on Contemporary Women's Theatre* (Ann Arbor, MI, University of Michigan Press, 1989), p. 282–97.

Castendyk, Stephanie, 'A Psychoanalytic Account for Lesbianism', *Feminist Review*, 42 (1992), pp. 67–81.

Chandler, Raymond, *Pearls Are a Nuisance* (Harmondsworth, Penguin, 1964).

Chesler, Phyllis, *Women and Madness* (New York, Doubleday, 1972).

Chodorow, Nancy, *The Reproduction of Mothering: Psychoanalysis and the Sociology of Gender* (Berkeley, CA, University of California Press, 1978).

Cixous, Hélène, 'The Laugh of the Medusa', in Elaine Marks and Isabelle de Courtivron (eds) *New French Feminisms: An Anthology* (Brighton, Harvester, 1981), pp. 245–64.

Cixous, Hélène, 'Sorties', in Elaine Marks and Isabelle de Courtivron (eds) *New French Feminisms; An Anthology* (Brighton, Harvester, 1981), pp. 90–8.

Colvin, Madeleine, with Hawksley, Jane, *Section 28: A Practical Guide to the Law and its Implications* (London, National Council for Civil Liberties, 1989).

Coote, Anna, and Campbell, Beatrix, *Sweet Freedom: The Struggle for Women's Liberation* (London, Picador, 1982).

Coward, Rosalind, *Patriarchal Precedents: Sexuality and Social Relations* (London, Routledge and Kegan Paul, 1983).

Coward, Rosalind, and Semple, Linda, 'Tracking Down the Past: Women and Detective Fiction', in Helen Carr (ed.) *From My Guy to Sci Fi: Genre and Women's Writing in the Postmodern World* (London, Pandora, 1989), pp. 39–57.

Cowie, Elizabeth, 'Fantasia' in Parveen Adams and Elizabeth Cowie (eds) *The Woman in Question: m/f* (London, Verso, 1990), pp. 149–96.

Culler, Jonathan, *On Destruction: Theory and Criticism after Structuralism* (London, Routledge and Kegan Paul, 1983).

Davis, Madeline, and Kennedy, Elizabeth Lapovsky, 'Oral History and the Study of Sexuality in the Lesbian Community: Buffalo, New York, 1940–1960', in Martin Bauml Duberman, Martha Vicinus and George Chauncey, jr. (eds) *Hidden from History: Reclaiming the Gay and Lesbian Past* (Sedona, AZ, American Library, 1989; Harmondsworth, Penguin, 1991), pp. 426–40.

Davis, Maggie, 'From Identity Politics to Scrambled Eggs', *The Pink Paper* (issue 265, 21 February 1993), p. 10.

Dollimore, Jonathan, 'The Cultural Politics of Perversion: Augustine, Shakespeare, Freud, Foucault', in Joseph Bristow (ed.) *Sexual Sameness: Textual Differences in Lesbian and Gay Writing* (London, Routledge, 1992), pp. 9–25.

Duncker, Patricia, *Sisters and Strangers: An Introduction to Contemporary Feminist Fiction* (Oxford, Blackwell, 1992).

Echols, Alice, 'The New Feminism of Yin and Yang', in Ann Snitow, Christine Stansell and Sharon Thompson (eds) *Desire: The Politics of Sexuality* (London, Virago, 1984), pp. 62–81.

Eisenstein, Hester, *Contemporary Feminist Thought* (London, Unwin, 1984).

Faderman, Lillian, *Surpassing the Love of Men: Romantic Friendship and Love between Women from the Renaissance to the Present* (London, Junction Books, 1981; London, Women's Press, 1985).

Faderman, Lillian, *Odd Girls and Twilight Lovers: A History of Lesbian Life in Twentieth-Century America* (New York, Columbia University Press, 1991; Harmondsworth, Penguin, 1992).

Farley, Pamella, 'Lesbianism and the Social Function of Taboo', in Hester Eisenstein and Alice Jardine (eds) *The Future of Difference* (Boston, MA, G.K. Hall, 1980), pp. 267–73.

Farr, Susan, 'The Art of Discipline: Creating Erotic Dramas of Play and Power', in SAMOIS (ed.) *Coming to Power: Writings and Graphics on Lesbian S/M* (Boston, MA, Alyson, 1982), pp. 181–9.

Felski, Rita, *Beyond Feminist Aesthetics: Feminist Literature and Social Change* (London, Hutchinson, 1989).

Fleenor, Juliann E. (ed.) *The Female Gothic* (Montreal, Canada, Eden Press, 1983).

Fletcher, John, 'Freud and His Uses: Psychoanalysis and Gay Theory', in Simon Shepherd and Mick Wallis (eds) *Coming on Strong: Gay Politics and Culture* (London, Unwin Hyman, 1989), pp. 90–118.

Forster, Margaret, *Daphne Du Maurier* (London, Chatto and Windus, 1993).

Franklin, Sarah, and Stacey, Jackie, 'Dyke Tactics for Difficult Times', in Christian McEwen and Sue O'Sullivan (eds) *Out the Other Side: Contemporary Lesbian Writing* (London, Virago, 1988), pp. 220–32.

Fraser, Jean, and Boffin, Tessa, *Stolen Glances: Lesbians Take Photographs* (London, Pandora, 1991).

Frith, Gill, *The Intimacy Which is Knowledge: Female Friendship in the Novels of Women Writers*, PhD Dissertation, University of Warwick, 1989.

Fuss, Diana, *Essentially Speaking: Feminism, Nature and Difference* (London, Routledge, 1989).

Gardiner, Judith Kegan, 'Mind Mother: Psychoanalysis and Feminism', in Gayle Greene and Coppelia Kahn (eds) *Making a Difference: Feminist Literary Criticism* (London, Methuen, 1985), pp. 113–45.

George, Sue, 'The Outsiders: Bisexuals', *The Guardian* (17 September 1991), p. 37.

Gillard, Frances, 'Letter', *The Guardian* (17 September 1992), p. 21.

Gregory, Deborah, 'From Where I Stand: A Case for Feminist Bisexuality', in Sue Cartledge and Joanna Ryan (eds) *Sex and Love: New Thoughts on Old Contradictions* (London, Women's Press, 1983), pp. 141–56.

Griffin, Gabriele (ed.) *Outwrite: Lesbian Popular Fiction* (London, Pluto, 1993).

Hamer, Diane, '"I am a Woman": Ann Bannon and the Writing of Lesbian Identity in the 1950s', in Mark Lilly (ed.) *Lesbian and Gay Writing: An Anthology of Critical Essays* (London, Macmillan, 1990), pp. 47–75.

Hamer, Diane, 'Significant Others: Lesbians and Psychoanalytic Theory', *Feminist Review*, 34 (1990), pp. 134–51.

Harris, Bertha, 'What We Mean to Say: Notes toward Defining the Nature of Lesbian Literature', *Heresies*, 3 (1977), p. 7.

Harris, Simon, *Lesbian and Gay Issues in the English Classroom: The Importance of Being Honest* (Milton Keynes, Open University Press, 1990).

Heath, Stephen, 'Joan Riviere and the Masquerade', in Victor Burgin, James Donald and Cora Kaplan (eds) *Formations of Fantasy* (London, Routledge, 1986), pp. 45–61.

Hermes, Joke, 'Sexuality in Lesbian Romance Fiction', *Feminist Review*, 42 (1992), pp. 49–66.

Hinds, Hilary, '*Oranges Are Not the Only Fruit*: Reaching Audiences Other Lesbian Texts Cannot Reach', in Sally Munt (ed.) *New Lesbian Criticism: Literary and Cultural Readings* (Hemel Hempstead, Harvester Wheatsheaf, 1992), pp. 153–72.

Hoagland, Sarah Lucia, and Penelope, Julia (eds) *For Lesbians Only: A Separatist Anthology* (London, Onlywomen, 1988).

Holmlund, Christine, 'The Lesbian, the Mother and the Heterosexual Lover: Irigaray's Recodings of Difference', *Feminist Studies,* 17(2) (1991), pp. 283–308.

Hull, Gloria T., Scott, Patricia Bell, and Smith, Barbara (eds) *All the Women Are White, All the Blacks Are Men, But Some of Us Are Brave: Black Women's Studies* (New York, The Feminist Press, 1982).

Humm, Maggie, *Feminist Criticism: Women as Contemporary Critics* (Brighton, Harvester, 1986).

Humm, Maggie, *Border Traffic: Strategies of Contemporary Women's Fiction* (Manchester, Manchester University Press, 1991).

Hutcheon, Linda, *The Politics of Postmodernism* (London, Routledge, 1989).

Irigaray, Luce, *Speculum of the Other Woman*, translated by Gillian C. Gill (New York, Cornell University Press, 1985). *(Speculum de l'autre femme*, Paris, Minuit, 1974).

Irigaray, Luce, *This Sex Which Is Not One*, translated by Catherine Porter with Carolyn Burke (New York, Cornell University Press, 1985). (*Ce Sexe qui n'en est pas un*, Paris, Minuit, 1977).

Jay, Karla, and Glasgow, Joanne (eds) *Lesbian Texts and Contexts Radical Revisions* (New York, New York University Press, 1990).

Jeffreys, Sheila, *The Spinster and her Enemies: Feminism and Sexuality 1880–1930* (London, Pandora, 1985).

Jeffreys, Sheila, 'Butch and Femme: Now and Then', in Lesbian History Group (ed.) *Not a Passing Phase: Reclaiming Lesbians in History 1840–1985* (London, Women's Press, 1989), pp. 158–87.

Johnston, Jill, *Lesbian Nation: The Feminist Solution* (New York, Simon and Schuster, 1974).

Juhasz, Suzanne, 'Towards a Theory of Form in Feminist Autobiography: Kate Millett's *Flying* and *Sita.* Maxine Hong Kingston's *The Woman Warrior*', in Estelle Jelinek (ed.) *Women's Autobiography* (Bloomington, Indiana University Press, 1980).

Kaplan, Cora, 'Radical Feminism and Literature: Rethinking Millett's *Sexual Politics*', in *Sea Changes: Essays on Culture and Feminism* (London, Verso, 1986).

Kaplan, Cora, 'An Unsuitable Genre for a Feminist?', *Women's Review*, 8 (1986), pp. 18–19.

Kaplan, Cora, 'Feminist Criticism Twenty Years On', in Helen Carr (ed.) *From My Guy to Sci-Fi: Genre and Women's Writing in the Postmodern World* (London, Pandora, 1989), pp. 15–23.

Kaplan, Rebecca, 'Compulsory Heterosexuality and the Bisexual Existence: Toward a Bisexual Understanding of Heterosexism', in Elizabeth Reba Weise (ed.) *Closer to Home: Bisexuality and Feminism* (Seattle, Seal Press, 1992), pp. 269–80.

Kawash, Samira, M., 'Macho Sluts: It's a White Thing?', paper given at the Fifth Annual Lesbian and Gay Studies Conference, Rutgers University, New Brunswick, November 1–3, 1991.

Kennedy, Maev, 'Two Sides to Sexuality', *The Guardian* (4 September 1992), p. 27.

Knight, Stephen, '"A Hard Cheerfulness": An Introduction to Raymond Chandler', in Brian Docherty (ed.) *American Crime Fiction* (Basingstoke, Macmillan, 1988), pp. 71–87.

Koedt, Anne, 'The Myth of the Vaginal Orgasm', in Anne Koedt, Ellen Levine and Anita Rapone (eds) *Radical Feminism* (New York Quadrangle, 1973), pp. 198–207.

Kramarae, Chris and Treichler, Paula A., *A Feminist Dictionary* (London, Pandora, 1985).

Kristeva, Julia, *Revolution in Poetic Language*, translated by Margaret Waller (New York, Columbia University Press, 1984).

Lechte, John, *Julia Kristeva* (London, Routledge, 1990).

Leeds Revolutionary Feminist Group, 'Political Lesbianism: The Case against Heterosexuality', in Onlywomen Press (ed.) *Love Your Enemy? The Debate between Heterosexual Feminism and Political Lesbianism* (London, Onlywomen, 1981), pp. 5–10.

Lewis, Reina, 'The Death of the Author and the Resurrection of the Dyke', in Sally Munt (ed) *New Lesbian Criticism: Literary and Cultural Readings* (Hemel Hempstead, Harvester Wheatsheaf, 1992), pp. 17–32.

Lilly, Mark, ed., *Lesbian and Gay Writing: An Anthology of Critical Essays* (London, Macmillan, 1990).

Little, Judy, *Comedy and the Woman Writer: Woolf, Spark and Feminism* (Lincoln, NB, University of Nebraska Press, 1983).

Lorde, Audre, *Sister Outsider: Essays and Speeches* (Trumansberg, Crossing Press, 1984).

McDougall, Joyce, *Theatres of the Mind: Illusion and Truth on the Psychoanalytic Stage* (London, Free Association Books, 1986).

McEwen, Christian, and O'Sullivan, Sue (eds) *Out the Other Side: Contemporary Lesbian Writing* (London, Virago, 1988).

McGuire, Scarlett, 'First Comes Prejudice', *The Guardian* (25 April 1988), p. 16.

McKenna, Neil, 'You're a queer: What school is like when you're gay', *The Guardian* (25 November 1991), p. 14.

MacNair, Mike, 'The Contradictory Politics of SM', in Simon Shepherd and Mick Wallis (eds) *Coming on Strong: Gay Politics and Culture* (London, Unwin Hyman, 1989), pp. 147–62.

March, Caeia, 'The Process of Writing *Three Ply Yarn*', in Elaine Hobby and Chris White (eds) *What Lesbians Do in Books* (London, Women's Press, 1991), pp. 239–55.

Marks, Elaine, and Stambolian, George, *Homosexualities and French Literature: Cultural Contexts/Critical Texts* (Ithaca, NY, Cornell University Press, 1979).

Merck, Mandy, *Perversions: Deviant Readings* (London, Virago, 1993).

Millett, Kate, *Sexual Politics* (1970) (New York, Avon, 1971).

Mitchell, Juliet, and Rose, Jacqueline (eds) *Feminine Sexuality: Jacques Lacan and the Ecole Freudienne* (London, Macmillan, 1982).

Mitchell, Juliet, *Psychoanalysis and Feminism* (New York, Pantheon, 1974).

Modleski, Tania, *Feminism Without Women: Culture and Criticism in a 'Postfeminist' Age* (London, Routledge, 1991).

Moi, Toril, *Sexual/Textual Politics: Feminist Literary Theory* (London, Methuen, 1985).

Munt, Sally, 'The Inverstigators: Lesbian Crime Fiction', in Susannah Radstone (ed.) *Sweet Dreams: Sexuality, Gender and Popular Fiction* (London, Lawrence and Wishart, 1988), pp. 91–119.

Munt, Sally (ed.) *New Lesbian Criticism: Literary and Cultural Readings* (Hemel Hempstead, Harvester Wheatsheaf, 1992).

Nestle, Joan, *A Restricted Country* (Ithaca, New York, Firebrand, 1987).

Nielsen, Sigrid, 'Strange Days', in Christian McEwen and Sue O'Sullivan (eds) *Out the Other Side: Contemporary Lesbian Writing* (London, Virago, 1988), pp. 93–106.

Oakley, Anne, and Mitchell, Juliet (eds) *The Rights and Wrongs of Women* (Harmondsworth, Penguin, 1976).

Off Pink Publishing (eds) *Bisexual Lives* (London, Off Pink Publishing, 1988).

Onlywomen Press (ed.) *Love Your Enemy? The Debate between Heterosexual Feminism and Political Lesbianism* (London, Onlywomen, 1981).

Palmer, Gerry, *Thrillers: Genesis and Structure of a Popular Genre* (London, Edward Arnold, 1978).

Palmer, Paulina, *Contemporary Women's Fiction: Narrative Practice and Feminist Theory* (Hemel Hempstead, Harvester Wheatsheaf, 1989).

Palmer, Paulina, 'Contemporary Lesbian Fiction: Texts for Everywoman', in Linda Anderson (ed.) *Plotting Change: Contemporary Women's Fiction* (London, Edward Arnold, 1990), pp. 43–62.

Palmer, Paulina, 'Antonia White's *Frost in May*: A Lesbian Feminist Reading', in Susan Sellers (ed.) *Feminist Criticism: Theory and Practice* (Hemel Hempstead, Harvester Wheatsheaf, 1991), pp. 89–108.

Palmer, Paulina, 'The Lesbian Feminist Thriller and Detective Novel', in Elaine Hobby and Chris White (eds) *What Lesbians Do in Books* (London, Women's Press, 1991), pp. 9–27.

Palmer, Paulina, 'The Lesbian Thriller: Crimes, Clues and Contradictions', in Gabriele Griffin (ed.) *Outwrite: Lesbianism and Popular Culture* (London, Pluto, 1993).

Pickering, Bobby, 'Queer Street Fighters', *The Guardian* (8 September 1992), p. 17.

Radford, Jean (ed.) *The Progress of Romance: The Politics of Popular Fiction* (London, Routledge and Kegan Paul, 1986).

Radicalesbians, 'The Woman Identified Woman', in Anne Koedt, Ellen Levine and Anita Rapone (eds) *Radical Feminism* (New York, Quadrangle, 1973), pp. 240–5.

Radway, Janice A., *Reading the Romance: Women, Patriarchy and Popular Literature* (Chapel Hill, NC, University of North Carolina Press, 1984).

Reed, Christopher, 'Judge persuaded to suspend Colorado's "anti-gay law" ', *The Guardian* (16 January 1993), p. 15.

Rich, Adrienne, *Of Woman Born: Motherhood as Experience and Institution* (New York, W.W. Norton, 1976; London, Virago, 1977).

Rich, Adrienne, *On Lies, Secrets and Silence: Selected Prose 1966–1978* (New York, W.W. Norton, 1979; London, Virago, 1980).

Rich, Adrienne, 'Compulsory Heterosexuality and Lesbian Existence', *Signs* 5(4) (1980), pp. 631–60, reprinted in Rich, *Blood, Bread and Poetry: Selected Prose 1979–1985* (London, Virago, 1987), pp. 23–75.

Riviere, Joan, 'Womanliness as Masquerade', in Victor Burgin, James Donald and Cora Kaplan (eds) *Formations of Fantasy* (London, Methuen, 1986), pp. 34–61.

Roberts, Michèle, 'Write, she said', in Jean Radford (ed.) *The Progress of Romance: The Politics of Popular Fiction* (London, Routledge and Kegan Paul, 1986), pp. 221–35.

Roelofs, Sarah, 'Section 28: What's in a Law', *Spare Rib*, 92 (June 1988), p. 42.

Roller, Judi, M., *The Politics of the Feminist Novel* (New York, Greenwood Press, 1986).

Roof, Judith, *A Lure of Knowledge: Lesbian Sexuality and Theory* (New York, Columbia University Press, 1991).

Rose, Jacqueline, *Sexuality in the Field of Vision* (London, Verso, 1986).

Rubin, Gayle, 'Thinking Sex: Notes for a Radical Theory of the Politics of Sexuality', in Carole S. Vance (ed.) *Pleasure and Danger: Exploring Female Sexuality* (London, Routledge and Kegan Paul, 1984), pp. 267–319.

Ryan, Joanna, 'Psychoanalysis and Women Loving Women', in Sue Cartledge and Ryan (eds) *Sex and Love: New Thoughts on Old Contradictions* (London, Women's Press, 1983), pp. 196–209.

SAMOIS (ed.) *Coming to Power: Writings and Graphics on Lesbian S/M* (1981; Boston, MA, Alyson, 1982).

Schulman, Sarah, 'Troubled Times: Interview by Andrea Freud Lewenstein', in Betsy Warland (ed.) *Inversions: Writing by Dykes, Queers and Lesbians* (Vancouver, Canada, Pressgang Publishers, 1991; London, Open Letters, 1992), pp. 217–26.

Sedgwick, Eve Kosofsky, *Epistemology of the Closet* (Hemel Hempstead, Harvester Wheatsheaf, 1991).

Smyth, Cherry, *Lesbians Talk Queer Notions* (London, Scarlet Press, 1992).

Snitow, Ann, Stansell, Christine, and Thompson, Sharon (eds) *Desire: The Politics of Sexuality* (London, Virago, 1984), first published as *Powers of Desire: The Politics of Sexuality* (New York, Monthly Review Press, 1983).

Symons, Julian, *Bloody Murder: From the Detective Story to the Crime Novel: A History* (Harmondsworth, Penguin, 1972).

Valverde, Mariana, *Sex, Power and Pleasure* (Toronto, Canada, The Women's Press, 1985).

Vance, Carole, S. (ed.) *Pleasure and Danger: Exploring Female Sexuality* (London, Routledge and Kegan Paul, 1984).

Walker, Nancy A., *A Very Serious Thing: Women's Humor and American Culture* (Minneapolis, MN, University of Minnesota Press, 1988).

Weise, Elizabeth Reba (ed.) *Closer to Home: Bisexuality and Feminism* (Seattle, WA, Seal Press, 1992).

White, Chris, 'Letter', *The Guardian* (17 September 1992), p. 21.

Whitford, Margaret, *Luce Irigaray: Philosophy in the Feminine* (London, Routledge, 1991).

Wilson, Anna, 'Investigating Romance: Who Killed the Detective's Lover?' paper given at the Fifth Annual Lesbian and Gay Studies Conference, Rutgers University, New Brunswick, NJ, 1–3 November, 1991.

Wilson, Anna, 'Lesbian Gumshoes', *Bay Windows*, 6(7) (18–24 February 1988), pp. 1–2.

Wilson, Elizabeth, 'Gayness and Liberalism', in Sandra Allen, Lee Sanders and Jan Wallis (eds) *Conditions of Illusion: Papers from the Women's Movement* (Leeds, Feminist Books, 1974), pp. 110–25.

Wilson, Elizabeth, 'I'll Climb the Stairway to Heaven: Lesbianism in the Seventies', in Sue Cartledge and Joanna Ryan (eds) *Sex and Love: New Thoughts on Old Contradictions* (London, Women's Press, 1983), pp. 180–95.

Wilson, Elizabeth, 'The Context of "Between Pleasure and Danger": The Barnard Conference on Sexuality', *Feminist Review*, 13 (1983), pp. 35–41.

Wilson, Elizabeth, 'Deviant Dress,' *Feminist Review*, 35 (1990), pp. 67–74.

Wilson, Elizabeth, with Weir, Angela, *Hidden Agendas: Theory, Politics and Experience in the Women's Movement* (London, Tavistock, 1986).

Wings, Mary, 'Lesbian Gothic – Victim or Victor?', paper given at the 'Activating Theory' Conference, University of York, 9–11 October 1992.

Wittig, Monique, 'One is Not Born a Woman', in *The Straight Mind and Other Essays* (Hemel Hempstead, Harvester Wheatsheaf, 1992), pp. 9–20.

Wolfe, Susan J., 'Ingroup Lesbian Feminist Political Humor', paper given at the Midwest Modern Language Association, Minneapolis, MN, November 1980.

Young, Stacey, 'Breaking Silence about the "B-Word": Bisexual Identity and Lesbian-Feminist Discourse', in Elizabeth Reba Weise (ed.) *Closer to Home: Bisexuality and Feminism* (Seattle, WA, Seal Press, 1992), pp. 75–87.

Zimmerman, Bonnie, 'What Has Never Been: An Overview of Lesbian Feminist Criticism', in Gayle Greene and Coppelia Kahn (eds) *Making a Difference: Feminist Literary Criticism* (London, Methuen, 1985), pp. 177–210.

Zimmerman, Bonnie, *The Safe Sea of Women: Lesbian Fiction 1969–1989* (Boston, MA, Beacon Press, 1990; London, Onlywomen, 1992).

Zimmerman, Bonnie, 'Lesbians Like This and That: Some Notes on Lesbian Criticism for the Nineties', in Sally Munt (ed.) *New Lesbian Criticism: Literary and Cultural Readings* (Hemel Hempstead, Harvester Wheatsheaf, 1992), pp. 1–15.

Zita, Jacquelyn N., 'Historical Amnesia and the Lesbian Continuum', in Nannerl O. Keohane, Michelle Z. Rosaldo and Barbara C. Gelpi, (eds) *Feminist Theory: A Critique of Ideology* (Chicago, IL, University of Chicago Press, 1981; Brighton, Harvester, 1982), pp. 161–76.

Index

LESBIAN AND GAY ISSUES IN THE ENGLISH CLASSROOM
THE IMPORTANCE OF BEING HONEST

Simon Harris

This book aims to examine aspects of sexuality as they pertain to contemporary English teaching. It begins by examining how it is that sexuality has found its way onto the educational agenda, concentrating particularly on the impact of Section 28 of the Local Government Act 1988 and the advent of health education relating to HIV and AIDS.

The book then looks at how lesbian and gay students currently fare in our schools before turning to the amenability of the subject English as a means of integrating issues of sexuality into the curriculum. This is then developed by an examination of how each level of the education system could best deal with the issue, paying particular note to the proposals for the National Curriculum and taking in the role of both Media Studies and Drama.

There then follows two schemes of work, one relating to Timothy Ireland's *Who Lies Inside* and the other to *Annie on my Mind* by Nancy Garden. Each consists of a six week unit suitable for GCSE course work based around the novel, making use of a range of additional materials.

The final section examines the role of the individual teacher dealing with the issue in isolation, a department acting on their own and the place of whole school policies. There is then a discussion of the rights and responsibilities of lesbian and gay teachers and the usefulness of positive images.

The appendix to the book consists of an annotated list of novels, plays and poems which might be of use in raising the issue.

Contents
Introduction − Why sexuality needs to be tackled − Why English? − Possible strategies − Case study 1: Who Lies Inside *by Timothy Ireland − Case study 2:* Annie on my Mind *by Nancy Garden − Splendid isolation or in concert? − Where to from here? − Appendix − Bibliography − Index.*

160pp   0 335 15194 9 (Paperback)

GIRLS AND SEXUALITY
TEACHING AND LEARNING

Lesley Holly (ed.)

Sexuality does not remain outside the school gates. It is part of life in schools as it is in the rest of society. This book explores some of the issues concerning sexuality and schools from the perspectives of girls and women.

The first section is called 'What should we teach about sex?' The chapters in this section raise questions about the way sex education is taught in schools. Are girls getting the information they need to preserve their health and avoid pregnancy? Is the information given in appropriate ways so that they can respond without embarrassment and really understand what it means to them? These kind of questions are considered through case study, study research and through teachers' accounts of their work.

In the second section 'Reflecting on our experiences', pupils, parents, teachers and researchers discuss the experience of being female in mixed state schools. How is women's sexuality reflected by and in schools? Not unexpectedly some of the answers concern silence, embarrassment and sexual harassment.

The contributors raise important issues about the sexual agenda of schooling. They reflect on some of the ways in which women's sexuality is distorted, neglected or rejected. They suggest not only that schools reflect the oppressive sexual attitudes of the wider society but that they are deeply implicated in its maintenance.

Contents
Introduction: the sexual agenda of schools – Section 1: What should we teach about sex? – Teaching sex: the experiences of four teachers – 'It makes you think again.' Discussing AIDS and other sexually transmitted diseases – 'Are you coming to see some dirty films today?' Sex education and adolescent sexuality – Child sexual abuse and the role of the teacher – 'My Nan said, "Sure you're not pregnant?" ' Schoolgirl mothers – Section 2: Reflecting on our experiences – Girls' experience of menstruation in school – Trying not just to survive: a lesbian teacher in a boys' school – 'A word might slip and that would be it.' Lesbian mothers and their children – The sexual harassment of young women – Appendix – Index.

Contributors
Isobel Gill, Jacqui Halson, Lesley Holly, Jenny Kitzinger, Lesbian Mothers Group, Lynda Measor and Shirley Prendergast.

160pp   0 335 09532 1 (Paperback)

THE POLITICS OF PLEASURE
AESTHETICS AND CULTURAL THEORY

Stephen Regan

For many years the study of aesthetics was regarded as a narrow and limited preoccupation, having only the slightest social and political relevance. With the advent of deconstruction, aesthetic considerations came to be seen not just as unfashionable but as deeply suspect and reprehensible. Within the growing realm of cultural studies, however, there is a strong and sustained revival of interest in questions of pleasure and value. The essays in this volume constitute a radical recovery and reappraisal of aesthetics and insist upon the continuing significance of aesthetic issues in modern culture. They address Marxist and feminist aesthetics, aesthetics and literary theory, modernism and postmodernism, pleasure and value. As well as surveying the aesthetic theories of Walter Pater, Roger Fry, Clive Bell, I.A. Richards, Roland Barthes, Paul de Man and others, these essays offer new and provocative interpretations of specific works of art. Among the writers whose works are discussed are William Wordsworth, Charles Baudelaire, Virginia Woolf, Franz Kafka, Samuel Beckett and Doris Lessing. Together, these essays welcome the return of the aesthetic as a powerful and productive idea in contemporary cultural politics.

Contents

Contributors
Michèle Barrett, Laurel Brake, Steven Connor, Terry Eagleton, Robin Jarvis, Adrian Page, Stephen Regan, Rebecca Stott, Geoff Wade, Patricia Waugh.

240pp   0 335 09759 6 (Paperback)